Surface Glaze & Form

Pottery Techniques

Surface Glaze & Form

Ceramic Arts Handbook Series

Edited by Anderson Turner

The American Ceramic Society
600 N. Cleveland Ave., Suite 210
Westerville, Ohio 43082

www.CeramicArtsDaily.org

The American Ceramic Society
600 N. Cleveland Ave., Suite 210
Westerville, OH 43082

© 2012 by The American Ceramic Society, All rights reserved.

ISBN: 978-1-57498-325-8 (Paperback)

ISBN: 978-1-57978-566-5 (PDF)

No part of this book may be reproduced, stored in a retrieval system or transmitted in any form or by any means, electronic, mechanical, photocopying, microfilming, recording or otherwise, without written permission from the publisher, except by a reviewer, who may quote brief passages in review.

Authorization to photocopy for internal or personal use beyond the limits of Sections 107 and 108 of the U.S. Copyright Law is granted by The American Ceramic Society, provided that the appropriate fee is paid directly to the Copyright Clearance Center, Inc., 222 Rosewood Drive, Danvers, MA 01923 U.S.A., www.copyright.com. Prior to photocopying items for educational classroom use, please contact Copyright Clearance Center, Inc. This consent does not extend to copyright items for general distribution or for advertising or promotional purposes or to republishing items in whole or in part in any work in any format. Requests for special photocopying permission and reprint requests should be directed to Director, Publications, The American Ceramic Society, 600 N. Cleveland Ave., Westerville, Ohio 43082 USA.

Every effort has been made to ensure that all the information in this book is accurate. Due to differing conditions, equipment, tools, and individual skills, the publisher cannot be responsible for any injuries, losses, and other damages that may result from the use of the information in this book. Final determination of the suitability of any information, procedure or product for use contemplated by any user, and the manner of that use, is the sole responsibility of the user. This book is intended for informational purposes only.

The views, opinions and findings contained in this book are those of the author. The publishers, editors, reviewers and author assume no responsibility or liability for errors or any consequences arising from the use of the information contained herein. Registered names and trademarks, etc., used in this publication, even without specific indication thereof, are not to be considered unprotected by the law. Mention of trade names of commercial products does not constitute endorsement or recommendation for use by the publishers, editors or authors.

Publisher: Charles Spahr, Executive Director, The American Ceramic Society

Art Book Program Manager: Bill Jones

Series Editor: Anderson Turner

Ebook Manager: Steve Hecker

Graphic Design and Production: Melissa Bury, Bury Design, Westerville, Ohio

Cover Images: *Gilded Pasture* by Steven Young Lee; (top right) *Swirls and Stripes* by Jason Bige Burnett; (bottom right) platter by Tim Ludwig (photo by Randall Smith).

Frontispiece: Vase by John Britt

Contents

When the Negative is Positive — 1
Ursula Hargens

Pour It On — 6
Sam Scott

Sarah Jaeger: Joyful Pots — 11
Emily Donahoe

Less is More — 16
Courtney Murphy

Second Childhood — 21
Linda Gates

Playing Dress-Up — 26
Magda Glusek

Slip Transfer — 33
Jason Bige Burnett

Slip and Sgraffito — 38
Kristin Pavelka

Layering Slips, Glazes and Decals — 43
Andrew Gilliatt

Elevating Earthenware — 49
Ben Carter

Forrest Lesch-Middelton: Layer by Layer — 53
Jeffrey Spahn

Paul Barchilon: Arabesque Designs — 57
Annie Chrietzberg

Designing for Food — 61
Gwendolyn Yoppolo

Making Bisque Molds — 67
Nancy Zoller

Marcos Lewis: Urchin Texure *Annie Chrietzberg*	**71**
Etched in Clay *Jim Gottuso*	**73**
Glaze Etching *Ann Ruel*	**77**
A Rainbow Revealed *Adrian Sandstrom*	**79**
Block Printing Stamps *Ann Ruel*	**83**
Grouting for Effect *Laura Reutter*	**87**
Word Decoration *Connie Norman*	**91**
A Painterly Approach *Tim Ludwig*	**95**
Using the Correct Brush *Michael Harbridge*	**99**
Chinese Brush Painting *Elizabeth Priddy*	**101**
Majolica Decoration *Jake Allee*	**107**
Expanding A Mid-Range Palette *Yoko Sekino-Bove*	**111**
Cone Six Celadons *John Britt*	**115**
Bristol Glazes *Cheryl Pannabecker*	**120**
Peach Bloom Glazes *John Britt*	**123**
Steven Young Lee: West to East and Back Again *Casey Ruble*	**131**

Preface

The focus of this book is not just on the surface of the object you make, but also on the complete design process. Many *Ceramics Monthly* and *Pottery Making Illustrated* articles have been chosen because they cover some part or all of the aspects of making a piece out of clay. One of my favorite artists whose work has been included in this book is Gwendolyn Yopollo. The article we have included details her consideration for the design, form and surface of an Orange Juicer. It is strong example of how clay artists can speak to formal aesthetic considerations while creating a utilitarian piece. It's also just a solid example of great ideas and great work. I hope it inspires you too.

This book marks the end of the Ceramic Arts Handbook series of twelve books and it felt right to have a broad approach to selecting articles for inclusion. As artists who focus on clay, we are not asked to do just one thing. We are walking and talking one-person companies in charge of developing our products, marketing and customer service. It has been the intention of this series of books to feed the soul of the artist. To give insights, but mostly to inspire your thought process in a new direction that will help you develop your ideas and keep you working. I like to imagine you taking one of these books into the studio, breaking the spine and using it as a resource for a project you are working on. I hope you have enjoyed these books as much as I have enjoyed helping to bring them to you.

Anderson Turner

When the Negative Is Positive

by Ursula Hargens

Wallflower (Reflection), 56 in. (1.4 m) in height, earthenware, glaze, fired to cone 05, gold luster, fired to cone 018. *Photo by Peter Lee.*

As the decoration on my thrown work has become more detailed and elaborate, I've begun looking to extend my decoration over larger surfaces. I chose wall tiles as a way to create large-scale compositions, treating the ceramic surface as a single canvas.

In designing my tiles, I set out to create standardized units that could be configured in multiple ways. My goal was to make tiles that were manageable but could be combined to create larger compositions. Altering the shape of a traditional square tile by manipulating the silhouette allowed me to create patterns with the tile forms themselves. I could use the same molds to make different shaped surfaces, giving me the ability to modify the overall size or orientation of a piece.

In my Wallflower series, I use two tile molds to create arrangements that reflect different compositional approaches—a repeating pattern and a single decorative pattern that spans the surface of the tiles. The cutouts in the tile provide an added challenge, requiring the surface decoration to respond to the empty spaces, corners, and edges created by the irregular shapes.

Making the Template and Mold

To make the tile mold, begin by cutting a positive model out of medium density fiberboard (MDF) using a table saw and jigsaw. Sand the model to create a slight angle so you can remove it after the plaster sets up, and apply several coats of polyurethane to seal it. Make a tile press mold by setting up wooden cottles in

MDF positive next to the finished plaster press mold.

Use a tarpaper template to cut a slab for the mold.

Add clay strips for the sides and reinforce with coils.

Apply one or more coats of white slip.

a square, clamping them, and filling the seams with clay coils. The cottles should be at least one inch from the edges of the MDF model. Then, secure the model so it won't move when the plaster is poured around it, coat it and the surrounding surfaces with Murphy's Oil Soap, and pour in enough plaster to cover the mold by at least one inch. After the plaster sets, remove the cottles, clean up the edges of the mold with a rasp, and dry it for several days (figure 1).

Pressing a Tile

To make a tile, roll a slab of clay ½-inch thick, and cut it in the shape of your tile. Use the MDF model as a guide or make a flexible template from cardboard or tarpaper (figure 2). Gently lay the slab into the mold and press the clay down, paying attention to the corners and edges as those are the areas often missed. Next, cut strips of clay to press into the sides of the mold and reinforce the seams with coils (figure 3).

Cover the tile with plastic and leave it overnight so that it sets up to leather hard. The next day, place a board across the mold opening and flip it over as you would flip a cake, so that the tile rests on the board. You may need to tap the mold with your fist to make the tile pop out. Clean up any rough edges with a rib.

5 Apply colored slip over the clay and paper resist.

6 Apply additional layers of slip design.

7 Poke holes through a paper design.

8 Make a pouncing sack.

9 Pounce the design.

Applying Slip

Coat the tile with a first layer of slip (figure 4). A white slip produces a light ground and brightens glaze colors, but any slip color can be used. Note the consistency of the slip and the wetness of the brush. If the slip is thin and applied in quick, single strokes, it appears translucent in places with the red clay showing beneath. If the slip is thicker (like cream) and applied in multiple strokes, it creates an opaque, white surface. You can also affect the way the slip lays on the surface through the wetness of the brush; a wet brush gives you a lighter, more fluid application and a dry brush pulls on the surface leaving a denser, slightly textured slip layer. Allow the slip to dry until the sheen is gone and it becomes firm to the touch.

Using Paper Resist

Now apply any secondary slip designs using paper resist techniques. I make colored slips by adding 10–20% stain to a white slip base, but any commercial underglaze or slip will work. Draw an image or shape onto newspaper. If you're going to repeat a design, make a master template out of heavier cardstock that you can trace if you need additional shapes. Use several pieces

Apply a glaze outline.

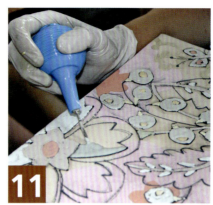
Fill in the outlines.

Pour clear glaze over the surface.

of newspaper so you're cutting multiple sheets at once. With scissors or a matte knife, cut an outline of the pattern. Keep both the positive and negative image intact so you have the option of using both the original shape and the outline in your design.

Lay the paper cutout on the surface and spray with a light mist of water to adhere it. Try not to use too much water as it can cause the white slip ground to moisten and smudge. Using your fingers, press the edge of the paper to the surface so there are no buckles or gaps around the edge of the design for slip to seep underneath. After all excess water from spraying has evaporated, apply colored slip, brushing from the perimeter inward (figure 5). Once the paper has been tacked to the surface by the slip, you can go back over it to create lines or texture with your brush. Wait for the slip to lose its sheen, and use a pin tool to lift up the paper from the surface, revealing the resist pattern (figure 6). This process can be repeated multiple times to extend a pattern or create a layered surface.

Dry the tiles slowly between layers of sheetrock (drywall) boards and put something heavy (the press mold itself works fine) on top to prevent warping. I bisque my tiles to cone 03 in an electric kiln.

Apply a Repeated Pattern

In order to repeat a glaze pattern multiple times, I use the Renaissance technique of pouncing. Trace the outline of the tile and pencil in a design for that tile shape. Then, perforate the paper by poking holes along the lines of the design with a pin tool (figure 7). This step is tedious, but once it's made, your outline can be used over and over again. When finished, lay the paper on top of a bisqued tile and rub a charcoal stick over the holes. I've found I get a darker outline using a pouncing sack that I make by pouring powdered graphite (available at most art supply stores) onto a small, cloth circle that is gathered and tied off with a string or twist tie to create a small bag (figure 8). Pat the sack over the pin-pricked design to release the powder through the holes (figure 9).

Once the pattern is pounced on the tile, trace the outline with a pencil to connect the dots and secure the pattern since the tile is often heavily handled in the glazing process and the pounced pattern can be easily blown away.

Applying Glaze

The first step to glazing is outlining the pattern. I use a black glaze that I mix in small batches at a thicker than normal consistency. You can also let a glaze stand for a few days with its lid off to thicken it through evaporation. The glaze is then put into squeeze bottles with needle tips and applied as a drawn line. You can buy squeeze bottles at ceramic supply stores or make your own (see box). I recommend using a 16 or 18 gauge nozzle.

The glaze line produced from the applicator creates a raised line, making a little wall of glaze (figure 10). The second step in glazing is to fill in the walled-off areas with colored glazes (figure 11). The glazes for this step should be a cream-like consistency so they flow into the walled-in reservoir and create an evenly glazed surface. If the glaze accidentally extends outside the desired area, it can be scraped off with a pin tool or small knife when dry.

Once all the areas are filled in with glaze and the surface is dry to the touch, brush liquid wax resist over the glazed areas. This keeps the glazes true to their original color and texture after the next step and prevents the design from running and blurring. After applying the wax, allow the pieces to stand overnight so that the wax resist dries fully and there's less clean-up.

The final glazing step is to dip, pour, or brush clear glaze over the surface (figure 12). This fills in background areas not covered by the colored glazes. I mix this glaze to a skim-milk consistency so it repels easily from the waxed areas. If it does cling to the waxed parts, remove it by dabbing with a damp sponge.

Firing and Hanging

After glazing, fire to cone 05 in an electric kiln. I bisque higher than I glaze fire to minimize pinholing and other glaze defects. After this firing, I frequently apply gold luster in small areas and re-fire the tile to cone 018.

Homemade Glaze Trailer

I use a homemade tool created from a nasal aspirator used for infants, a ball inflating needle, and a piece of masking tape. Clip off the end (approximately ½ inch) of the nasal aspirator so that you can just squeeze the inflating needle snugly in the opening. Inflating needles have a second small hole on the side; a small piece of masking tape wrapped around the end of the needle adequately blocks this hole. I like these homemade applicators because they are inexpensive, it is easy to replace the needle if it gets clogged, and I prefer the way the bulb feels—as if it's an extension of my hand.

Pour It On

by Sam Scott

Lidded jar, 14 in. (36 cm) in height, wheel-thrown porcelain, black glaze.

In the early 1970s, an encounter with Bob Sperry's work influenced my decision to go to the University of Washington. Sperry's on-glaze brushwork had attracted me and after three years there, in addition to facility with a brush and learning to work with porcelain, I had acquired many skills. Upon graduation, I set up my studio and began to develop my own approach to brushwork. One of my techniques was to leave areas of the porcelain surface unglazed. When I applied the oxides, I would get a different color depending on whether the brushwork was on clay or glaze. I applied the glaze by pouring it over selective areas, and with practice, I began to control the poured areas and was able create interesting patterns. The biomorphic shapes would widen or taper based on the flow of the glaze and the form of the piece being glazed.

As time passed, the patterns became more interesting, but given that I used a clear glaze, there was little contrast to the clay and glaze. My main focus was to add visual interest to the brushwork. In the 1990s, I began to develop a black matte glaze. Because this black glaze contrasted with the white porcelain, the patterns themselves became the main focus of the surface decoration.

Throwing the Container

After wedging, the clay is centered, opened up, and drawn into a cylinder for the body of the lidded container. The height and width of the cylinder is dictated by the actual form you are planning to make. My round forms tend to be more vertical, so the cylinders I start with are taller than they are wide.

Working with porcelain can be difficult, but I've found that my clay (Kai Porcelain from Laguna Clay Co.) has a window of workability where forming on the wheel is manageable. When too stiff, it's difficult to wedge and center; if it's too soft it has no body and slumps easily. Another reality of porcelain is the thickness that needs to be left in the lower region of larger round forms. The extra clay supports the curves.

As a result, trimming figures prominently when working in porcelain; the form one wishes to end up with will be the inside shape. After trimming the excess clay from the outside, you're left with the desired profile.

After the cylinder is made, I begin to nudge the central shape out with my middle finger on the inside and a flexible metal rib on the outside. As the curve develops, I change to a curved wooden rib on the inside that's sized to the scale of the piece while still using the metal rib outside (figure 1).

Once the basic form is achieved, I collar the shoulder into the desired diameter. On a lidded jar of reasonable size, I try to leave an opening that allows you to reach in with your hand. But the actual size is always dictated by the best proportions of lid to form. When the opening is correct, I create a flange for the lid by turning the edge of the clay up. Finally, I refine this area with a rib.

Capping it Off

Measuring and throwing the lid comes next. For a cap lid, this is basically a short cylinder or a bowl with straight walls. Use calipers to measure the diameter of the outside of the flange at the top of the pot (figure 2). This measurement should be the same or larger than the inside edge of the lid, which is thrown upside down as a low, wide cylinder (figure 3). I angle the flange slightly so the widest point is at the shoulder of the jar. The lid will actually sit on the jar's shoulder. Making the fit tighter allows for some adjustments while trimming. I can remove clay from the lid edge or flange to get the best fit. I've found that this style of lid should fit snug after the bisque as the flange shrinks a bit more than the lid in the glaze firing. At this point, the pieces are put aside to get evenly leather-hard. Depending on the size of the piece and amount of moisture in the air, this can take a few days.

Trimming the Form

Once the pieces reach a stiff leather hard, they're ready to trim. I primarily use a Kemper LT5 loop tool and keep the trimming tools very sharp for working on stiffer clay. If the clay sticks to the tool while trimming, it's too soft. For a round form with a small opening, I use a leather-hard chuck to support the piece while trimming. I prefer the clay-to-clay contact because there is a resistance to slipping that is not there with a bisque-fired chuck. I have found that with care, I can keep the chucks leather-hard for months or years and use them repeatedly.

I center the chuck, put the piece in it in an upright position, and center it. I use a pencil to make a line on the lowest part of the pot so it will be visible when turned upside down (figure 4). This mark is the refer-

Surface Glaze&Form

Black and white vase, 10 in. (25 cm) in height, wheel-thrown and handbuilt porcelain, black glaze.

1. Finish the jar's curve using a curved wooden rib on the inside and a flexible metal rib on the outside.

2. Measure the diameter of the outside of the flange using calipers.

3. Throw the lid as a low wide cylinder. Use the caliper measurement to size the inside diameter properly.

4. Mark a line around the lowest part of the pot as it sits in the chuck after it's leveled.

5. Jar placed upside down in the chuck, with the marked line level. The opening is parallel to the line.

6. Establish the diameter and interior of the foot then remove excess clay from the walls using a loop tool.

ence I use to ensure that the form is not skewed in the chuck. If I get the upside-down form centered in the chuck with the line level, I know the opening (which is not visible in this position) is parallel to the line and now centered (figure 5).

The Foot

When I'm satisfied that it's centered, I begin to trim. The first thing I do is establish the diameter of the foot. These round forms are designed to have feet so I can hold the piece firmly while glazing. It's important that the foot always be high enough and wide enough so that I can easily grasp the piece. I also find that these parameters make an effective foot for the visual balance I want.

As I continue to trim, I am aware of the thickness and continuity of form. After removing most of the excess clay with the loop tool (figure 6), I use a stainless-steel rib at

7 Shave the trimming marks using a metal rib held at close to a right angle against the pot.

8 Hold the metal rib against the pot at a low angle to smooth out the trimming marks.

9 Use a foam bat to trim the lid. This works for low, wide forms.

10 Apply the glaze using a combination of pouring and splashing from a flexible plastic container.

11 The shape of the pot, glaze viscosity, velocity and angling the pot changes the poured shape.

12 The finished pot, prior to glaze firing. Glaze was poured with the pot upside down as well as upright.

close to a right angle to shave the clay and remove the marks made by the loop tool (figure 7). After all the clay and marks are removed, I moisten the surface and quickly use that same rib, at a low angle, to get a very smooth but not burnished surface (figure 8). The piece is then put upright in the chuck and the upper area is smoothed as well. To trim the lid I use a foam bat, which is resistant to slippage with low, wide forms (figure 9). I make sure the bottom is flat, then turn it over (base down) to trim the edge if I need to fine tune the fit. I then trim it, edge down, to remove the excess clay.

Adding Handles

After trimming, the handles are applied. The form is usually too stiff after trimming, so I moisten it a bit before attaching the handles. These handles have a bone-like quality to them. When I began making these forms, I imagined them as reliquaries, so having bone handles seemed appropriate.

I pull the handle to the appropriate size, and when it is soft leather-hard, I push the cut end to flare it out and then smooth the edge. I need two of equal size. I then take three balls of clay and slip and score them to make a stand-off for the handle. I set a straight edge on top of the flange to show where to locate the handles, ensuring that they are not above the opening.

Making a Splash

Once the piece is bisque-fired to cone 09, it is ready to be glazed. All of my forms are smooth with uninterrupted curves, making surface decoration a bit easier. Whether I use brushwork or the pouring technique, throwing lines or variations in surface texture compete with and alter the decoration.

The technique I use is remarkably simple. I use a small, flexible margarine container with a thin edge so I can alter its width as needed to get a wider or narrower flow. As I begin to apply the glaze, it is a combination of pour and splash (figure 10). If I touch the container to the pot, it splits the flow of glaze. If I just splash it on the piece, I am not able to control the shape as the glaze flows down the surface. The angle at which I hold the pot, the shape of the piece, the viscosity of the glaze, and the degree of impetus I give the glaze at the initial pour all factor into the shapes that develop (figures 11 and 12). I also alter the angle

Lidded jar with brushwork and poured clear glaze, 10 in. (25 cm) in height, wheel-thrown porcelain, clear glaze.

and directionality (from the rim or from the foot) of the pours to create a graphic tension on the surface.

I pour from either the top or bottom in a fairly random manner to begin with. Once this area is dry, I pour from the other direction, reacting to the shapes that now exist on the surface, as shown in figures 11 and 12. At this point, I can see the pattern begin to energize the surface. The size of the biomorphic shapes, the distance between the shapes, whether they touch or not, all factor into the effect. When I am finished pouring, I scrape off the inevitable small splatters with a needle tool and use an eraser to clean off any residue. Because of the fluidity of the poured shapes, I rarely alter them. If I get an edge I don't like, I pour over that area to clean it up.

Sarah Jaeger
Joyful Pots

by Emily Donahoe

Sarah Jaeger's simple, well designed serving bowl brings both ood and cheer to the dinner table.

Geometric patterns and forms combine with organic, plant-inspired lines in artist Sarah Jaeger's inviting functional pots. In her hands, a modest, wheel-thrown serving bowl becomes something special with some easy alterations and a layered, wax-resist glazing technique.

The alterations developed over years of playing around with simple geometric forms—dividing up the space, making rounds into squares, and just seeing where things went.

"A lot of the evolution just comes from working on the wheel and doing something and then thinking, well, what would happen if I tried this?" she explains. "So it doesn't start out as high concept all the time."

Sarah says that the alterations are "both visual and tactile—and both of those things come into play with functional pots." Add to that Sarah's love of decoration and the surface of the bowl becomes a space where pattern and irregularity meet. She says her goal is to make a bowl that functions well, that's also beautiful and adds some joy and a sense of festivity to someone's meal. For her, it's about making things more joyful.

Throwing and Altering

Sarah's small but well-appointed backyard studio looks out onto a sunlit garden. Her dogs, Archie and Oona, laze nearby as she goes about her work.

"This is, in many respects, a very simple pot," says Sarah as she centers a 4½-pound lump of clay on the wheel in preparation for making a serving bowl. She is working with porcelain, which she prefers because of its translucent quality. "With porcelain, even when the pot is unglazed or even if it is a monochrome glaze, you get a lot of interesting play of light and shadow that I think is very beautiful," she explains.

Throwing the bowl starts out normally, the clay is centered, opened to the desired depth and diameter. When making the initial center hole, Sarah purposefully leaves more clay in the floor of the pot. By not pressing down as far when creating this hole, she leaves room for trimming a taller foot on the pot. Then, she starts to pull up the walls.

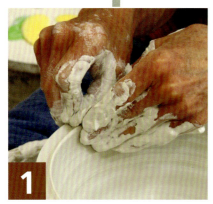

1 Define the split rim using the back of your thumb pressed down in the middle.

2 Use ribs on the inside and outside to compress the walls and remove throwing lines.

3 Refine the split rim using a wooden knife or rib while supporting the rim on both sides as you work.

4 Divide the rim using a circle divider and marking tool. Press in at each mark, creating six lobes.

5 Refining and smoothing the trimmed surface using a rubber rib to remove any lines or marks.

6 Draw a design on the inside of the freshly glazed pot using a pencil.

To create the flange on the exterior of the bowl, she pulls up the wall of the pot halfway and then skips a vertical space of about an inch and a half, resuming the pull just above it. This leaves a thicker area that can be trimmed to shape later. She then splits the rim using the back of her thumb pressed lightly into the middle (figure 1).

Next, she goes back to refine the shape of the bowl. As she works, she explains the process. "I did about two or three pulls with a sponge in my outside hand and then I go to using ribs (figure 2). I use the curve of the rib to help me get the inside curve of the bowl; but also the ribs really help to compress the clay and make it stronger. After a few pulls with your hands, if you go and use the rib, it strengthens it, recompresses it. It also gets rid of all the throwing lines. Sometimes (the marks are) something you want to use visually and sometimes they're just distracting."

The split rim is further refined using a wooden knife (figure 3). Using a sponge, Sarah cleans up the slurry from the inside of the bowl, then uses a thin piece of plastic to smooth out the rim.

Surface Glaze & Form

7 After painting in the leaf forms using a colored wash, trail on green glaze line decorations.

8 Additional red glaze decorations are trailed on next. The trailed glaze should be thicker so it does not run.

9 Use a tinted wax resist to visibly protect the painted and trailed patterns and shapes.

10 After the wax dries, paint a layer of wash, here copper sulfate, over the surface to create another layer.

The bowl is ready to be altered. Sarah drops a small circle divider into the bottom of the bowl as a guide and uses a chopstick to divide the rim into six sections. Next, at each mark or divot, she presses the chopstick into the wall from the flange to the top, creating six lobes (figure 4).

Trimming

When the bowl is leather-hard, Sarah centers and secures it for trimming. For heavier pieces, or pieces with very uneven rims, she uses a foam covered bat.

"I intentionally leave quite a depth of clay here, just because I want this pot to have a really nice, elevated foot. I want to be able to work with the proportions of the lip element and the volume element and then the foot, so a little extra clay leaves me some leeway to play with."

Using a trimming tool, Sarah removes excess clay from the bowl. As she trims, first creating the outer diameter of the foot and then the inside diameter, she taps the area she's working on every once in a while to gauge its thickness. She then trims another flange to echo the one she's thrown into the bowl. After she's achieved the shape she wants, Sarah removes excess clay until the bowl is of the right heft.

"I'm pretty fussy about the weight of the pots," says Sarah. "There's something about the way a pot looks that sets up an expectation for what it's going to weigh. With a bowl that I intend to be a functional pot, my goal is not to mess with people's expectations about what it is or how it functions."

After trimming, she goes over the surface with a rubber rib to smooth out any lines from the tool, and to refine the transition between the rounded bottom and the outer flange (figure 5).

Decorating

Sarah works atop the New York Times Arts and Travel sections—after she's read the articles, of course. She wears latex gloves to protect her hands from the abrasive glaze. After waxing the foot of the bisque-fired bowl with paraffin, she uses tongs to dip the bowl into a clear glaze, allowing it to dry for a bit before beginning the first step in decorating.

"This is another one of my secret tools: it's a no. 2 pencil," Sarah explains as she draws a simple leaf pattern inside the bowl (figure 6), and then uses a paintbrush to fill in the patterns with a wash of rutile and Gerstley borate. She applies a thin layer for a translucent, cloudy effect (see figure 7).

As she works, Sarah explains that her decorations have evolved out of hand repetition and "responding to the curve of the pot."

"A lot of my glaze decorations started out as very geometric patterns and over the years evolved into more botanical patterns. The longer I did it . . . the more organic the lines and the forms and those decorative motifs became," says Sarah. "I like patterns that are pretty organized and symmetrical but then, when the pot gets fired everything softens and relaxes. There's a kind of nice contradiction there."

The next two glazes are applied in thick, dense lines. The first is Reeve Green, mixed very thick to give the bowl some texture (figure 7). Sarah applies the glaze using Clairol color applicator bottles, which she gets at a beauty supply store. She then uses the same technique with an orange-red glaze, which is made from the same base glaze as Reeve Green, but with red inclusion stain added (figure 8). On the outside of the bowl, Sarah uses the same elements in a different arrangement; she decorates the bowl all the way down to the underside of the foot, filling in the spots between leaves with simple waves and crosshatches.

"It's a three-dimensional pot," says Sarah. "I think it matters to pay attention to all of it." Plus," she adds, "when people wash dishes, they love that the undersides are decorated. One time this guy in California emailed me a photo of bowls in the dishwasher."

Wax and Wash

Wax resist is an old technique, but Sarah finds that she uses it a little bit differently than most potters.

"One thing that caused me to keep playing with this technique is that I really love surfaces that have a sense of depth," says Sarah. "It confuses that figure-ground relationship—and for some reason that confusion really interests me."

Sarah uses a color-tinted Aftosa wax to go over the decorations on the bowl with a Japanese-style brush (figure 9). This type of wax helps her to see what she's done and also brushes on more easily than paraffin wax.

"The wax will repel anything that goes on over it. Some other waxes that flow and brush well don't seem to resist the cobalt sulfate as well as Aftosa," explains Sarah. "So I will paint with wax on all the parts of this that I want to remain what they are now."

Sarah's final step is to brush a cobalt sulfate wash over the entire bowl (figure 10). She mixes the colorant with water by eye, testing it on newsprint to see that it is the right concentration before applying it. Sarah explains, "The form of cobalt sulfate that I use, because it's water-soluble, you get a really soft line. Just like when a watercolor goes on paper and it bleeds into the paper, as the water of the cobalt sulfate wash evaporates, the cobalt bleeds into the glaze, so the line quality is really soft." Note: Cobalt sulfate, like all soluble salts is easily absorbed into the skin. It is important to wear latex gloves when working with this, or any other soluble salt colorant. It is not recommended to use this material in group studio situations.

As she finishes up the pot (figure 11), Sarah reflects on the paradox of spending so much time discussing technique—and so much time decorating a single pot. "At the end, you don't want the person who is using the pot to think about technique at all. You don't want it to look like it was a lot of work; you just want it to look like itself."

Recipes

Reeve Base
Cone 10 (oxidation or reduction)

Custer Feldspar	75 %
Whiting	15
EPK Kaolin	5
Silica	5
	100 %
Add: Bentonite	2 %
Green: Chrome Oxide	4 %
Red: Cerdec Intensive Red	10 %

Used as the trailing overglaze colors. When trailing this glaze, it needs to be thick so that it does not run.

Limestone Clear
Cone 10 (oxidation or reduction)

Custer Feldspar	27.0 %
Ball Clay (OM 4)	14.0
EPK Kaolin	7.0
Whiting	20.5
Silica	31.5
	100.0 %

This glaze is not an absolute clear. On its own in reduction, it's a little greenish.

Less Is More

by Courtney Murphy

Combining clean lines and spare but playful decoration gives Courtney Murphy's work an inviting, slightly retro feel.

I've always been drawn to spare and simple forms, and much of my time is spent looking at textiles, artwork, and household items from the mid-20th century. I have a deep appreciation for simple, well-designed industrial objects, as well as children's artwork and folk art—things that are less refined and show the hand of the maker. In my work, I attempt to seek a balance between these two interests. I strive for the clean lines and gracefulness, while my drawings and color choices are more influenced by children's artwork and folk art. The simplicity of the form creates a canvas for a more playful element in the drawing.

Making a Big Switch

For many years I worked with a white mid-fire clay. I used underglazes, drew incised lines, and created areas of color on a white background. I liked the work that I was making, yet it didn't really feel like me. It felt too clean and precise.

During this time, I would often take classes and workshops focused on earthenware. It was fun to work on a larger scale, to work a little more loosely, coil building new forms and trying out new surface decoration techniques. I liked the option of working on a larger scale that earthenware provided, and often thought about switching over, but at the end of each class or workshop, I would always return to my white clay, where I felt more comfortable.

I spent one fall assisting Jerilyn Virden at Penland School of Crafts. Jerilyn creates beautiful double-walled forms using earthenware. Living at Penland for two months,

Surface Glaze & Form

1 Applying terra sigillata to the foot of a bowl.

2 Burnishing the terra sigillata with a plastic grocery bag.

3 Cleaning glaze off of the bottom with a sponge.

4 Using a drywall screen to sand out glaze drips.

and working with earthenware every day provided me with the right incentive to change my clay body as well as my style of work. It was a bit of a bumpy transition, as I tried to learn a new palette of glazes and surface decorations, but at the end of two months, I had a few pieces that seemed promising.

That winter, I left for Montana to begin a two-year residency at the Archie Bray Foundation. Once I arrived, I immediately started testing slips and glazes. I really loved Posey Bacopoulos' cone 04 satin majolica recipe. At Penland, we had been working with earthenware in the 02 to cone 2 range, and Posey's glaze was beautiful at cone 01—no longer satiny, it looked more like enamel. I'd originally envisioned using a satin glaze, but I liked the way my drawings fused into the surface of the glaze at a higher temperature.

Waste Not, Want Not

After all of those years working in white clay, I had a huge supply of underglazes. I didn't want the jars to go to waste, so I started testing all of my colors over the majolica to see what would happen. A surprising number of the underglaze colors looked great, those that didn't were very dry or bubbled. I put a big 'X'

Using an 18-gauge slip trailer to draw lines on a bowl.

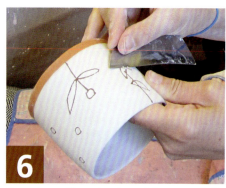
Scraping off a mistake with a metal rib.

Painting with underglaze over majolica.

Glazing and Decorating

After the work has been bisqued to cone 04–05, I begin glazing. I don't use wax, mainly because I'm pretty clumsy with it. Instead I scrape the excess glaze off with a rubber rib, then sponge the rest off, leaving about ¼ inch of the clay exposed on the bottom (figure 3). To cut down on drip marks, once the glaze has dried a little, I use a soft drywall screen to sand out the larger drip marks. I always wear a dust mask and sand while holding the piece away from myself and over a bucket of water to minimize dust (figure 4).

Because the glazing and decorating process takes a while, glazing is done in small batches. I using three different colored versions of my base glaze: yellow, pale mint green, and white. I try to focus glazing with one color at a time, otherwise it gets confusing, as all of the glazes look the same in the bucket. This helps me to avoid touching up a piece with the wrong color.

When I first switched to majolica, I knew that I would miss the preci-

on those and boxed them up, so that I wouldn't accidentally use them. The colors I use are mainly Amaco Velvet underglazes and Duncan underglazes. Testing is required as certain colors will work fine, but a similar shade won't work. I often mix the colors that do work to create new shades.

After switching to earthenware, I started brushing two to three thin layers of a terra sigillata on the bottom of bone-dry work to enhance the color of the clay and create a nicer feel on the bottom (figure 1). Once the sig has lost its sheen, I burnish it by wrapping a plastic grocery bag tightly around my thumb and rubbing the coated area (figure 2).

Finished creamer and sugar with yellow majolica glaze.

sion of the incised lines, but found that an 18-gauge slip-trailing bottle creates a very nice, fine line (figure 5). A 16-gauge bottle will form a thicker line. I use this less often, but it is useful for drawing dots on pieces. I fill the bottle with underglaze and add water if needed to get a smooth flow. Before drawing on a pot, test that it's flowing evenly on a piece of paper. Globs do happen occasionally, but they're easy to clean if you let them dry then scrape them off using a metal rib (figure 6). After scraping, rub out that spot with a finger and redraw the line.

There is definitely a window of time when this process works best. I start drawing lines on top of the majolica about a half an hour after glazing. Line drawing comes fairly easily as long as the glaze doesn't get too dry and powdery. Once it has reached this stage, the slip trailer does not flow as easily. Lightly misting the glazed piece with water sometimes helps, but it's much better to decorate while the glaze still has some moisture in it.

When not in use, I plug the slip-trailing bottles with a sewing pin (the type with a little bead on the end). This works really well, and it's nice to have the pin available in case the tip gets clogged. It's important

Lidded jar, earthenware, majolica glaze, trailed and painted underglaze decoration, fired to cone 01.

to remember to keep the pin in the tip when the bottles aren't in use, because they dry out easily.

The line drawings dry really quickly. Usually I'll draw on five to six pots, then start coloring in my drawings (figure 7). For the painting stage, I find it easier to pour my underglazes into a plastic ice tray, preferably one with a lot of compartments. The empty compartments are good for mixing underglaze colors together.

Drawing Inspiration

My drawings aren't planned out beforehand; I tend to work more intuitively, looking at the space and seeing how I want to divide it up. I've spent the last two years trying to find the right balance between too little and too much decoration.

My drawings are mostly inspired by the idea of connection. I have moved a lot over the past several years and being in a residency situation involves a lot of people moving in and out of your life. Some of these connections have stayed very strong despite the distances. My drawings often occur in groupings of two to three similar elements, dotted lines sometimes connect these elements, creating lines of communication.

I'm also intrigued by the new connections that are formed when a pot leaves my studio to become a part of somebody else's life. I find this to be one of the most interesting aspects of being an object maker. Using pots made by friends who are far away really does help me to feel connected to them. It's a really nice part of being a potter.

Recipes

Mel's Fantastic Sig

1 Part Redart
2 Parts distilled water

Add: 0.025% Darvan 7 based on the clay weight, not of both the clay and water combined.

1. Blunge Darvan into water.
2. Slowly add clay to water and blunge for about 3–5 minutes.
3. Ball mill for 12–24 hours (no longer or shorter).
4. Pour into clear container, let sit for 12–18 hours.
5. Either siphon out middle layer, or just pour off the top 2 layers. The top layer of water should be minimal so its not usually worth siphoning.
6. Simmer gently on the stove, stirring constantly, until the mixture reduces itself to about $2/3$ its original volume. If a skin forms on the surface while you're simmering it, just mix it back in. Save all chunks of clay.
7. When the sig cools, use a brush to re-integrate all the chunks and the liquid sig. There should be a slight sheen on the surface and the material should brush smoothly onto bone-dry pots.

I realize this is a more elaborate sig recipe than others you might have seen. I've tried simpler recipes, but had a lot of problems with flaking or weird textures. Finally my friend Mel Griffin gave me this recipe and it's worked really well.

PB Matte Majolica
Cone 05–01

Dolomite	10 %
Ferro Frit 3124	65
EPK Kaolin	20
Silica	5
	100 %
Add: Zircopax	10 %

Although this glaze was formulated to be a satin matte at cone 05, I have been firing it to cone 01. To tint the glaze I add between 1–6 percent Mason stain.

Surface
Glaze&Form

Second Childhood

by Linda Gates

The distressed or worn surface treatment and nostalgic images of paper dolls on Linda Gates' works transport the viewer (and artist) to a different time.

For the last year, I've used images of the paper dolls I remember from my 1950s childhood as the primary focus of my ceramic work. The idea started with my final year's project in the ceramic design program at Bath Spa University in England. I decorated ceramic surfaces using commercial digital decals with imagery of everyday objects from the 1950s, including the paper dolls of that era. Just before graduating, I set up my studio with an electric kiln, a table, and a couple of shelves so I could continue working. Though my studio is small (7×13 ft.), I've found that digital technology and the ability to order custom-made decals of my own designs has made it possible for me to continue and expand upon the investigations started while I was a student.

Image Sources

I use a combination of my drawings and found images to create my surface designs. I search for vintage dolls in my local city of Bath and further afield at book fairs, vintage fairs, antique toy shops, and online auctions. The ephemeral nature of paper dolls means that few have survived. However, some were carefully packed away into attics, and see the light of day again when the attics are cleared (figure 1). Many of the lovingly played-with dolls are tattered and torn and need repair or new clothes drawn for them. For this, I use a combination of sketches and Photoshop images (figure 2).

It's important that the dolls evoke the period and match the ones of my childhood memories. As they can be difficult to find, I often draw the dolls and dresses using inks and watercolor paints and pencils.

Life in the 1950s was not yet dominated by blatant consumerism, and I want my work to reflect this time of simple, carefree pleasures. By introducing text with messages such as 'No Batteries Required', I'm highlighting the contrast with the electronic toys of today.

Designing Decals

The decals I use are commercially made from Photoshop documents of my scanned images. In the U.S.,

1 Vintage paper dolls used as image sources for custom ceramic decals.

2 Enhance and compile sketches and scanned images using Photoshop.

3 Sheets of custom printed decals created from Photoshop files.

companies like Bel Inc. and Easy Ceramic Decals will produce custom-made ceramic decals of your designs. In England, I've used Foto-Ceramic (see page 20 for website information). They are based in Stoke-on-Trent, the historic center of pottery manufacture in England.

Using Photoshop, scan the drawings, manipulate and enhance them, and finally put them together into an 8½×11 in. document and make sure the mode is set to CMYK for the color rather than RGB, and the resolution is print quality (at least 300 dpi). Most decal companies will accept documents sent via email attachment when you place your order. The finished, printed decals will then be sent to you in the mail. The paper backing sheets are printed with ceramic inks, then laminated with fritted sheets, which ensure the inks fuse into the glaze when fired (figure 3). To save space and money, many decals are printed on the same sheet of decal paper. To keep the decals organized, clean and dry, cut around each one and put them into individual envelopes until needed.

Casting a Form

Ceramic decals can be applied to any glazed object, but it makes life easier if the ceramic form has smooth surfaces to avoid the problem of trapped air creating bubbles and holes in the image. The ceramic form shown here is a slip-cast jug that I designed as part of a college tableware design project. With a little modification to the original jug design, I made new plaster molds, one for the body of the form and the other for the handle (figures 4 and 5). The mold for the body of the jug is made in four parts—the two sides, the base, and the reservoir.

To prevent leaks when pouring the casting slip, secure the parts firmly together with strong bands cut from rubber inner tubes. If you design your mold to include a reservoir, which makes it easier to maintain an even rim thickness, fill the mold to halfway up the reservoir wall using a commercial casting slip of your choice (figure 6). As the porous mold absorbs the water from the clay, the excess is drawn from the reservoir. The handle mold is also filled with

Surface
Glaze&Form

4 Four-part plaster mold used for slipcasting the jug form.

5 Plaster mold for the handle. The two openings allow air to escape.

6 Secure separate parts of a plaster mold before filling with casting slip.

7 Allow the forms to set up before removing them from the molds.

8 While the forms are leather hard, cover surface with a colored engobe.

9 Add border of underglazes to the surface, then bisque fire the piece.

casting slip. Once the slip is the desired thickness (check by blowing on the edge of the mold where the slip and plaster meet), pour the extra slip back into the container and leave the mold inverted at an angle to drain into a bucket. Placing it at an angle avoids stalactites of clay forming on the bottom of the piece. Tip: To achieve an even wall thickness in multiple casts, time the first casting and use this as a guideline for when to drain the slip each time.

When the mold is well drained and the sheen has gone from the wet casting slip (typically about 20 minutes), remove only the reservoir portion from the jug mold, trim the excess clay from the top and clean it up with a damp sponge. I leave the rest of the mold intact for another hour or so for the form to firm up for easier handling. Both molds are then disassembled and the jug form and handle carefully removed (figure 7). Both component parts are cleaned up with a fettling knife and damp sponge. The handle is attached, and the form is covered in plastic for 24 hours to ensure a secure join.

Decorating Techniques

At the leather-hard stage, I decorate the jugs with colored slips and give them borders of commercial underglazes (figure 8 and 9). When the jugs have been bisque fired to cone 04, I give them a wash of iron ox-

10 For a distressed or antique look, coat the forms with a thin wash of iron oxide.

11 Select and cut out a group of decal images for use on each glazed form.

12 Soak the decal in distilled water for a minute to release image from the paper backing sheet.

13 Prior to firing, the decal retains the color of the fritted laminate sheet (in this case blue). This color burns out.

ide to dirty them down and give a distressed look because otherwise the bare slip-cast surface is gleaming white (figure 10). This surface is further enhanced with underglaze crayons and pencils.

Once you've applied any underglaze decoration to your pieces, they're now ready for a coat of clear glaze and put into the kiln on stilts, if necessary, for firing. Decal transfer works best on shiny, smooth glaze surfaces, so keep this in mind when selecting a glaze. After glaze firing, the ware must be handled as little as possible as the surface must be clean and free of grease from fingerprints. To ensure this, wipe the surface with rubbing alcohol.

Decalcomania

Now comes the fun part—selecting, arranging, and applying the images (figure 11). Gather the cut-out decals you want to use together with a shallow tray and some distilled water, which is free of contaminants, a kitchen towel for blotting excess water, and a soft rib and natural sponge to smooth out any air bubbles. Soak the decal in the distilled water for about a minute until you can see the image start to release from the paper backing sheet (figure

Doll with Blue Underwear, 5 in. (12.5 cm) in height, slip-cast earthenware, slips, underglazes, oxides, and decals.

12). Carefully position the decal onto the dampened smooth glaze surface, gently slide away the backing paper from beneath the image, and smooth out the image using the soft rib or damp sponge. Once removed from its paper backing, the decal is very flimsy and must be handled with great care. There is a short opportunity to reposition the image and rub out any air bubbles using a rubber rib and a sponge while the transfer is still wet and before it dries and attaches itself to the glazed surface. At this stage, the decal will still retain the color of the fritted laminate sheet, which in my case is blue (figure 13). This burns out in the firing.

When all the decals are applied and fully dried, the jugs are ready for the final firing. Because it is just high enough to melt the glaze slightly, the ware must again be placed on stilts. During the firing, the fritted laminate will fuse the ceramic inks into the glaze, making them permanent. Cone 014 is the usual decal firing temperature, but reds do tend to burn out. To overcome this, I prefer to fire to approximately cone 015 with a 15 minute soak to make sure the inks fuse into the glaze. Note: Always check with the decal manufacturer for the appropriate firing temperature. As always in ceramics, it is very important to test as kilns and materials vary. The kiln used for decal firings must be well ventilated. Make sure all vents are open, and if you have a ventilation system attached to the kiln, be sure to turn it on when firing decals. The fumes are toxic so the room must also be well ventilated and the kiln preferably fired when there is no one around. I have discovered that I can add more layers of decals and fire the piece again as long as the subsequent firing does not to exceed the original decal firing temperature.

With very little equipment—a small kiln, a computer, and a bucket of clear glaze, I am having fun enjoying my second childhood.

Ordering Your Own Custom Digital Ceramic Decals

United States suppliers
Bel Inc. (beldecal.com)
Easy Ceramic Decals
(www.easyceramicdecals.com)

UK supplier
FotoCeramic (www.fotoceramic.com)

South African supplier
 (ships internationally)
JT McMasters (www.skolldecal.com)

Playing Dress-Up

by Magda Gluszek

Magda Gluszek's animated figures tell open ended stories through pose, expression, and brightly colored confectionary surfaces.

My clay sculptures investigate ideas about consumption, self-presentation, and societal behaviors versus animalistic impulses. Using the building solid and hollowing out technique allows flexibility in planning dramatic, performative poses while a combination of ceramic and mixed media surfaces give me a variety of options for referencing confectionary textures and colors. I'm constantly absorbing information about multimedia processes from hardware stores, craft books, and other artists that add depth and variety to my figures.

Getting started

Building solid forms in clay is a technique often looked at as a means to an end and not an end in and of itself. It's traditionally used by artists who take a mold from their sculptures and cast them in another material such as bronze or iron. I strive for a gestural style in my sculptures, leaving my tool marks as evidence of how I work, a style influenced by artists such as Auguste Rodin as well as my studies of terra-cotta maquettes from the 1700s and 1800s for larger works in clay, marble or bronze.

I begin by sketching and then building a small maquette to work out the positioning of a figure and details of the pose. The small models have a life to them that's very different from the polished quality of the finished works. It's important to capture that fresh feeling and liveliness in my figures. Trans-

Surface Glaze & Form

1 Measure the maquette and mark a scaled-up outline on the work surface.

2 Press wooden dowels into the solid clay wherever support is needed.

3 Use a plastic, putty knife to create gestural marks and imply an underlying structure.

4 Remove the head and model it separately to ensure refined details and facial expression.

5 The details of the fingers and hand are also modelled separately, before being reattached.

6 Stamp patterns into the surface. Use cornstarch as a release.

lating the sketches to a three-dimensional model is essential to the building process because it helps me to adjust the pose and proportions of the figure as well as plan the final scale of the piece. Measuring the maquette and marking out the workspace gives me an idea of the sculpture's final dimensions, in this case four times greater than the maquette (figure 1). This also allows me to check myself throughout the building process by measuring various parts of the body and comparing them to the model.

Creating the sculpture

The mass of the sculpture is built up with solid clay. Wooden dowels are added wherever support is needed and clay is squeezed around them to hold them in place and extend the form (figure 2). These linear extensions are also planted to determine the direction and angle of limbs. The maquette is referenced constantly throughout this process. Wherever possible, dowels protrude beyond the form for easy removal. As limbs begin to extend further from the figure, external dowels are added for extra support. Because the clay

7 Cut the appendages with a wire tool when pre-leather hard. Make registration marks on each half.

8 Hollow out the limbs so the wall is an even thickness, then score the edges and reattach.

9 After the head is hollowed, cut an access opening in the back for inserting the eyes.

10 After removing and hollowing the limbs, the torso is ready to be hollowed out.

11 Cut sections from the torso, hollow out, then reassemble using the registration marks as guides.

12 Attach the hollowed out limbs, using supports as necessary until the piece firms up.

dries and shrinks around the internal supports, the strength of each limb is constantly monitored and I remove the dowels as soon as the limb can support itself or be supported externally.

Initially, clay is added and manipulated by hand, but as the form progresses I use a plastic putty knife to direct the material, imply the underlying bone and muscular structure and create gestural marks. Building solid allows me to work the form as a whole and gives me the flexibility to fluidly correct proportions and change direction of limbs (figure 3).

Details

Detailing the sculpture begins once the whole body is roughed out. As the form gains definition, I switch to smaller wooden and plastic knives to make more specific markings and delineate skin folds. Detailed areas of the figure, such as the head and hands, are removed from the body and modeled separately (figures 4 and 5). When completed, they are reattached to the form. Thin and exposed limbs are covered to prevent them from drying too quickly.

A commercial sprig mold and home-made stamps add decorative

13 Add appendages that need to be positioned specifically after all other parts have been joined.

14 Apply white terra sigillata to the legs and pink terra sigillata to the upper body.

15 Paint the figure with a mixture of Gerstley borate and commercial stains.

16 Trail a satin-matte glaze that's mixed with a deflocculant to create raised, icing-like line patterns.

17 Mix epoxy resin with crushed chalk pastels to create the illusion of a sugary syrup.

18 Add confectionary sprinkles to the resin in the indented stamped area.

elements which have an aesthetic quality contrasting my gestural hand and tool markings. I make stamps by attaching decorative mirror findings and upholstery tacks to thick wooden dowels (figure 6).

Cornstarch is used as a release agent in the mold and dusted on the figure, preventing the plastic stamps from sticking and allowing them to make clear impressions. The cornstarch leaves no trace when fired.

Hollowing

After the figure is completely modeled, I allow it to dry to a stage that is slightly soft-leather hard. Extending limbs are wrapped loosely with plastic because they dry quickly. When these appendages reach the right stage, I assess where to make the first cut to begin hollowing, usually starting with a hand or a foot, providing it does not compromise the balance of the figure. I cut with a wire tool, aiming for a spot with minimal detail to repair upon reattachment. Notches are made around the cut so that the pieces can later be matched up to their exact position (figure 7). Various sizes of loop tools are used to dig out the interior clay until the walls reach a consistent

Apply epoxy putty around the eyeballs. This will secure them to the eye sockets.

Insert the eyes through the opening in the back of the head and position them appropriately.

Epoxy the access point at the back of the head using epoxy putty.

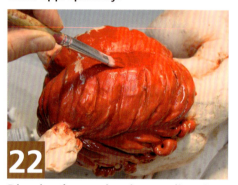

Disguise the repair using acrylic paint that's mixed to match the red glaze.

thickness of about ¼ inch. A wooden knife is used to compress the inside walls for added strength.

Each time a section is hollowed, it is wrapped in plastic and placed on a piece of foam to prevent distortion. When two sections are hollowed I score the edges with a homemade tool composed of several sewing needles epoxied to the end of a wooden dowel (figure 8). Slip is applied and the forms are rejoined. Fresh clay is worked into both interior and exterior seams. I try to recreate the markings of the initial building process while disguising the connection.

The arms, legs, and head are removed and re-built piece by piece in this manner. They are then wrapped and laid aside on foam. When hollowing the head, I remove the eyeballs, leaving empty sockets. A section is cut away from the back of the head (figure 9), allowing access to install porcelain eyeballs, post-firing.

Next, hollow out the solid torso (figure 10) and reassemble it in the same manner as the head, hands, and legs (figure 11). Begin by attaching the limbs first (figure 12). Appendages that require specific positioning, like the hands, are added last (figure 13). The attachments are often fragile and limbs are propped with various supports and clay.

Magda's surface detail shows her seamless integration of traditional and multimedia decoration techniques.

Cover the entire piece with plastic for several days, unwrapping it a little each day and allowing it to dry evenly. Finishing

My work takes advantage of both ceramic materials and mixed media when creating the confection-referencing surfaces. Along with traditional surface treatments like terra sigillata, glaze, and colored stains, I use paste and resin epoxies, oil paint, acrylic paint, chalk pastels, microfilament, candy sprinkles, paste wax, and other materials as they relate to my concepts.

Fired Finishes

When the figure is nearly bone dry, I apply a coating of white terra sigillata to the legs and terra sigillata colored with pink Mason stain to the upper body (figure 14). The sculpture is bisque fired to cone 06.

After the bisque firing, I prepare several commercial stains with Gerstley borate and paint them in concentrated areas to accentuate the sprigging and stamps (figure 15). Excess stain is removed with a damp sponge. Three brush coats of red glaze are applied to the hair and the piece is fired to cone 03.

For the final firing, a satin matte glaze is mixed with several color variations and sieved through a 100 mesh screen. A few drops of sodium silicate deflocculate it and lessen the amount of water necessary to make it flow. This causes the glaze to retain a raised quality when trailed over the form using an ear syringe fitted with an inflating needle (figure 16). Under-firing the glaze to cone 08 allows it to retain a raised, semi-matte quality, similar to icing.

Post-firing Finishes

When the glaze firing is done, I fit the figure with eyeballs. I prefabricate several porcelain eye shapes using Helios Porcelain from Highwater Clays, Inc., fire them separately to cone 7, and attach them postfiring. The contrasting clay bodies and separation of the eyes from the form creates a dramatic and realistic expression. I paint the eyes with oil paints, thinned with linseed oil. The iris color is chosen to match the figure's red hair, then other highlight colors are added. A needle tool is used to detail the iris by dragging through lighter values of paint and creating highlights.

While the paint is drying, I add resin to selected parts of the figure, coloring it to resemble sugary syrup.

Recipes

Red Earthenware

Talc	9 %
Ball Clay (OM4)	9
Fire Clay (Hawthorn)	14
Goldart	9
Redart	59
	100 %

Pete Pinnell No Ball Mill Terra Sigillata

Water	3 cups
Ball Clay (OM4)	400 g

Mix ingredients in a blender. Add sodium silicate drop by drop until the mix thins. Let sit for 48 hrs. Keep the top 1/3 and discard remaining material.

Pink Sigillata

1 cup sigillata
3 tsp. Mason Stain (MS) 6020 Pink

Red Icing Glaze
Cone 03

Whiting	10 %
Ferro Frit 3124	50
Kona F-4 Feldspar	40
	100 %

Add:
Mason Stain 6026 Lobster .... 25 %

Colored Stain

1 part Mason Stain
3 parts Gerstley Borate

Green: MS 6242 Bermuda
Blue: MS 6364 Turquoise Blue
Red: MS 6026 Lobster
Pink: MS 6020 Pink

Val Cushing Transparent Satin Glaze
Cone 03 (fired to Cone 06)

Gerstley Borate	17 %
Whiting	3
Ferro Frit 3124	52
Kona F-4 Feldspar	15
EPK Kaolin	2
Silica	11
	100 %

Add:
Green: MS 6242 Bermuda .... 5 %
Blue: MS 6364 Turquoise Blue ..... 5 %
Yellow: MS 6404 Vanadium .... 15 %

Wearing gloves and a respirator that protects against volatile organic fumes, I mix equal parts of resin and hardener, and stir vigorously. A coating is painted over the eyes to protect the oil paint and add luminosity. Fine shavings of chalk pastels can be added to tint the resin a variety of colors. I pour it into the figure's mouth as well as various indentations formed by the stamps (figure 17). Confectionary sprinkles are embedded into the resin for further decoration (figure 18). Small pieces of microfilament are placed between the figure's fingertips and mouth and coated with resin to give the illusion of dripping.

After the resin cures overnight, I mix a small amount of two-part East Valley Epoxy putty which can easily be modeled to mimic clay and apply it to the eyes (figure 19). They are carefully inserted into the sockets and positioned appropriately (figure 20). The figure is turned face-down while the epoxy cures, preventing the eyeballs from shifting. This allows me to attach the fired clay cover over the access point at the back of the head with more East Valley Epoxy putty and disguise the repair with acrylic paint (figures 21 and 22).

To complete the sculpture, a coating of paste wax is brushed on to the figure's flesh. When dry, it can be lightly buffed with a cloth to give the skin a soft sheen.

Slip Transfer

by Jason Bige Burnett

Too Much Television, uses newsprint and slip decoration combined with incised decoration, decals, luster, and glaze, creating dimensional surfaces that also pop with color.

My childhood interest in television cartoons influenced my current ceramic forms and surfaces. The bright colors, graphic patterns, and illustrative qualities recapture and celebrate my fascination with whimsical domestic representation. I'm inspired by the stylized hand-drawn utilitarian objects like a coffee mug in a cartoon character's hand or the mixing bowl displayed on the shelf in their kitchen.

The combination of commercial stained slips and newsprint create a stick-and-peel process. By applying slips saturated with bold colors onto newsprint, then transferring the drawn images to a slipped clay object, I can achieve an animated surface. Playtime doesn't end there; I continue by introducing stamps, stains, and stickers to further enhance the ceramic surface until the desired effect is fully achieved.

Creating Newsprint Transfers

The process I'm using is equivalent to making a monoprint in traditional printmaking. Instead of drawing on a metal plate and transferring the image to paper, I'm drawing on newspaper then transferring to clay. As with all monoprints, keep in mind that the image you create will be reversed. Text must be backwards and layers of color must be applied foreground to background (figure 1). Whether it be stripes, shapes, illustrations, or a color field, start with an idea of how you would like to approach the surfaces of your piece before you start.

Apply your pattern or drawing to strips or blocks of newsprint, varying the colors of slip using brushes, slip trailers, and sponge stamps. Use caution as the paper causes the slip to dry; and if it dries too much, it may chip off. Use a spray bottle to keep the image damp but don't spray

Circus Stars and Stripes, 7 in. in height, earthenware, slip, underglaze, glaze, iron-toner decals, and gold luster.

too much water, as it could puddle and smear the slip. The local newspaper works well but I prefer using Strathmore brand Newsprint Paper available at any art supply store. The thickness and tooth of this paper is durable and tough enough to hold and transfer slip.

Slip it and Stick it

After you've completed the newsprint image, wait for the slip to become leather hard and then apply a slip coat over the drawing. Lightly dab the first coat of slip on (figure 2), wait for this coat to become leather hard and then brush on a second coat. A hair dryer assists in getting the slipped newsprint to leather-hard. If the slip has a glossy shine then it's too wet to continue.

The slip application works best on leather-hard clay. Using a hake brush, apply a moderate coat of slip to the surface. This layer of slip shouldn't be too thin or too thick and it should be the consistency of heavy whipping cream. This slip coat creates a tactile surface perfect for pressing newsprint into and absorbs transferred slip and imagery well.

When the slip-coated clay piece and the slip decoration on the newsprint are both at leather hard, you are ready to print. There is a narrow window of time here where the surface of your piece and the newspaper are perfect for application. If one or the other is too wet when applied, the result could be sloppy and undesirable. If the image and object are too dry, then this affects the quality of adhesion. When the slip on the object is soft but not tacky and all the slip on the paper has lost its sheen, you're ready to transfer the image.

Carefully pick up your piece of newsprint and slowly bring it toward the object. You'll see the image through the newsprint and that assists with placement. Once any part of the newsprint transfer touches the object, gently press the rest of the newsprint onto the surface (figure 3). Note that air pockets result on curved surfaces. These are addressed later. Gently press the transfer onto the surface with your hands, working over the general area. The trapped air pockets can be removed by piercing them with a needle tool or a small X-Acto blade. If the air pockets are not taken care of, they can cause defects or misprinting of the transfer.

Now that the newsprint has been applied to the object, there's a layer

1. Create patterns with colored slips. Paint the foreground layer first and the background last.

2. When leather-hard, blot and brush on the background slip which also serves as a transfer coat.

3. Gently apply the newsprint to the piece. Use a soft rib to ensure contact and pierce any trapped air.

4. When the slip has had time to absorb and the newsprint has lost a lot of its moisture, slowly peel it away from the surface.

5. Apply damp newsprint strips to the surface and press down all edges to prevent the second slip coat from seeping underneath.

6. Brush additional slip coats over both the first layer and the damp newsprint strips. Use any color or combination of colors you wish.

of moisture trapped between the object and the paper. Within the first minute or two the clay object begins absorbing that moisture.

Using a soft rib, press the newsprint down, applying more pressure than before. Between thirty seconds and two minutes is about the time when you'll notice the newsprint drying out again. Take a slightly harder rib and, with more force than before, rub the newsprint one last time into the clay. Rubbing too hard could smudge the slip underneath or tear through the paper. Practice and experience with this method is the best way to find your limits.

Grab a corner or take the edge of the newsprint and slowly begin to peel away (figure 4). It's important to do this slowly so you'll catch the spots that did not adhere to the surface. Just place it back down gently and massage the spot down into the surface with the medium-soft rib. Repeat if necessary. Not addressing the spots creates potential reservoirs for stain and glazes later. Now that your image is transferred, handle the piece carefully. Applying slip onto leather-hard clay will make the clay soft and malleable again. I suggest waiting until your piece becomes firm and the slip isn't sticky

7 Create more of a tactile surface by applying another layer of thick slip onto a fresh piece of newsprint and wrapping it around the object.

8 After allowing the slip to absorb into the surface for a minute or two, peel away the newsprint again to reveal the varied, textured surfaces.

9 Mark the surface with stamps, rollers and carving tools, creating new patterns and echoing the lines of the form or of the colored bands.

10 Take advantage of the piece being leather hard and carve away some larger areas of the slip, revealing the contrasting color of the clay.

11 After the work has been bisqued, apply underglaze or stain over the object and wipe away to accentuate the process marks.

12 Apply soda ash wash, wax resist, and glazes to desired surfaces. This is the time to plan for a final layer of decals and lusters.

to the touch before applying anything else to the surface.

Additional Decorations

If you want a contrasting decorations in an adjoining area, apply another coat of slip to the leather-hard clay. This time, try cutting out stripes or shapes of plain newsprint, spritz with water until slightly damp, and lay them over the slip coat to act as a stencil resist (figure 5). Brush over the piece with another slip, again any color works, and let sit until the slip firms up (figure 6).

On top of the slip and strip layer, I also like creating built up textures of slip. Brush a moderate coat of slip onto a wide strip of newsprint and vary the thickness of application. Once leather hard, place the wide strip over the slip-coated object with the newsprint stripes still in place (figure 7). Be more relaxed with this and just gently pat down the strip. Give it a variation of rubs and pressings, then peel away and notice the loose quality and nature of the slipped surface (figure 8). Any sharp edges of slip should be tapped down or pressed in with your fingers. After this surface has been bisqued, stains and washes enhance the loose look, suggesting surfaces such as torn wallpaper or chipped paint.

Next, carefully peel the stripes away. If locating the paper and peeling it away is difficult, lightly heat the surface with a blow dryer until the slip above the newsprint becomes noticeably different in color and dryness. Now the paper can be removed with the aid of a needle tool or an X-Acto blade.

Stamp it Out

Since the object is still leather hard after the newsprint and resist techniques, more adornment may be applied. You can create additional marks using stamps, drawn in lines, and texture rollers (figure 9). Larger areas of slip can also be carved away and create more surface depth (figure 10).

Layering After the Bisque

Staining the work with an underglaze creates more depth and enhances the process marks and indentations previously made on the surface. Coat the entire piece with one or two layers of underglaze, let dry, and sponge it away from the high points leaving it in the recesses (figure 11). I use a black underglaze to give my work a distressed look and to enhance all the intricate marking made up until this point. Let the underglaze dry prior to applying wash and glazes.

Tip: Since the whole object will not be covered in glaze, some areas will remain matte. If the matte surfaces remain untreated they come out looking chalky and dry. To prevent this, apply a soda ash wash over the piece in two generous brush coats. To make the soda ash wash, combine 57 grams of soda ash to 1 cup of heated water and stir to dissolve the ingredients. Allow the piece to dry again. The soda ash wash will cause the matte surfaces to retain a moist and saturated look. I fire the stains, glazes, and soda ash wash together to cone 05–04, and then do a second firing of the iron toner decals to cone 08, finally I do a third firing of gold luster and commercial decals together to cone 017. I've fired the soda ash wash up to cone 2 but not past that.

I use a variety of shop-made and commercial glazes. For many, glazing is the last and final step, but I find glaze firing is only an intermediate step when pushing surfaces even further. When glazing, try setting up areas for decals and lusters by selectively applying the glaze (figure 12). Remember, decals and lusters reflect the surface below them and work best when applied to a shiny surface.

Swirls and Stripes, 10¼ in. (26 cm) in diameter, earthenware, slip, underglaze, glaze, iron-toner decals, commercial decals, and gold luster, 2011.

Recipes

All Purpose White Slip
Cone 04-10

Ferro Frit 3124	19.2%
EPK Kaolin	27.0
OM4 Ball Clay	27.0
Silica	21.4
Zircopax	5.4
Total	100.0%

Add: Mason Stains

Mason stain percentages vary per color. Try testing within the range of 3–10% to start.

Slip and Sgraffito

by Kristin Pavelka

Tidbits and more! Kristin Pavelka's patterned plates may have different motifs, but the drawn shapes and layers of colorful satin glazes complement one another so well that they can be mixed and matched, just like your favorite appetizers.

I fell in love with red earthenware after viewing the Iranian sgraffito wares of the 11th and 12th centuries in the Freer Gallery in Washington, D.C. I enjoyed the casual application of glaze as it moved beyond its established etched boundaries or dripped down the sides of the outside wall. The pots displayed a depth and softness of surface that I was excited to utilize in my own work while putting a contemporary spin on these beautiful historical pots. My current work blends ideas from these Iranian wares as well as sugary confections, mid-century and Scandinavian patterns, personal surroundings, and the styling of Martha Stewart.

Throwing the Plates

To make a 9-inch diameter plate, I start with 3½–4 pounds of clay. Working on a bat, I center the lump of clay into a low disk, wheel wedging a few times to work in some moisture if the clay is a little stiff. To open the form, I use the pinky side of my right hand in a "karate chop" position (figure 1). I continue to open and compress the clay with the pads of my fingertips until I've formed a desirable curve for the plate (figure 2). A stiff rubber or steel rib is lightly pushed into the clay, working from the inside to the outside to finish compressing and to alleviate the peaks and valleys formed from my fingertips (figure 3).

1 To open the plate form, I use the pinky side of my right hand in a "karate chop" position.

2 Continue to open and compress the clay with the pads of your fingertips until you've formed the inner curve.

3 Using a stiff rib, press lightly into the clay to finish compressing it and to remove the ridges.

4 Compress and re-center the rim before every pull to avoid cracks and unevenness.

5 Lightly run a stiff rubber or steel rib to lay down the rim and create a gentle curve.

6 Trim out the interior of your foot ring, starting from the center and working out.

The wall of the plate is now ready to be thrown. Before every pull, compress and re-center the rim (figure 4) to correct any wobbles. My right index finger forms a hook and the side of the first knuckle presses in on the opened clay at the base until the wall lifts slightly. Then with equal pressure from the right hand and left fingertips I gently squeeze the clay at the base and follow the small bulge all the way through the lip of the plate, easing up on the pressure as I get to the lip but sill following through. The wall is pulled up at a 45° angle (visible in figure 4). This is repeated two or three more times until the desired wall thickness is achieved. I make sure that the base of the plate stays wide and that the bottom of the wall is slightly thicker than the top to support its weight. This support structure will be trimmed away later, so I don't worry if it seems too thick. Before adjusting the angle of the rim, I use a wooden knife to cut off the skirt of clay at the base of the plate.

Using a rib, lightly run it from the center to the rim of the plate one or two more times, gently laying down the rim and creating a gradual curve across the bottom (figure 5). Carefully cut the base with a taut wire and let the plate dry to leather hard for trimming.

Ceramic Arts Handbook

7 Pour white slip onto the middle of the plate, turning the piece clockwise until the entire face is covered.

8 Scratch through the slip so that the tool just barely digs into the underlying clay.

9 Brush the surface once the design is complete to clean up the edges of the incised lines.

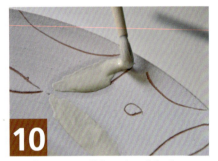
10 Load up a small brush with the darker-toned glaze and fill in the pod shapes on the bisque-fired plate.

11 Once the first glaze is dry, apply a coat of a lighter-toned satin glaze using the same technique as for pouring the slip.

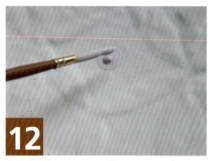
12 Apply the accent glazes, starting with the lighter glaze, and finishing with small dots of darker glaze.

Trimming the Foot

Get reacquainted with the form of your plate, feeling the thickness of the wall and bottom, so you know where to trim as well as how much to take off. Center and attach the plate to the wheel head with a few lugs of soft clay. Using a wide-edged trimming tool (I use the Dolan 310 pear tool) trim the profile of the plate first. I like a foot that is wide enough to support the plate when being cut upon, but narrow enough that it gives the pot a nice visual lift. Once the plate's profile and the outer edge of the foot are established through trimming, draw the inside circumference of the foot ring with a needle tool, and trim out the interior, starting from the center and working out to your line (figure 6). Level the foot ring if needed and compress the bottom of the foot to create a smooth surface on which the pot will sit. Carefully remove the attaching lugs of clay and, keeping the plate centered, lightly trim the edge of the plate so the profile has a continuous flow.

Slip and Sgraffito Decoration

I slip my pots when they look dry but have a small bit of moisture in them. This allows for a relatively even coating of slip, yet it dries a bit slower giving me time to complete my sgrafitto before the slip starts to chip when scratched. Because the slip dries quickly, I have to work fast to complete my design, so I plan the patterns ahead of time in a sketchbook or by drawing with a soft pencil on the unslipped plate itself.

Once I've decided on a pattern, I can begin slipping. Holding the plate vertically, I pour the white slip onto the middle of the plate using a large ladle, turning the piece clockwise until the entire face is covered (figure 7). Keep the plate vertical until the slip drips have firmed, then rest the plate on the tabletop and allow the slip to dry for a few minutes until you can touch it without a fingerprint remaining, but while it still feels cold and damp.

Lightly draw a grid on the piece using a soft pencil. Breaking up the space symmetrically on a circular form is a quick and easy way to understand the space. I sometimes draw my pattern on the piece to double check the placement of key elements, but usually I draw directly with my sgraffito tool using just the grid as an aid for placing the design.

My sgrafitto tool had a previous life as a dentistry tool and is thicker and duller than a standard needle tool. A long nail with a dull point is a good substitute. The line created is thicker than an X-Acto blade or needle tool and can give a similar line quality as a standard-sized pencil lead. Medium pressure is exerted with the tool tip so that it scratches through the white slip and just barely digs into the red underlying clay (figure 8). I brush a stiff yet soft-bristled brush across the surface of the plate once the design is carved to clean up the edges of the incised lines as well to rid the surface of the slip crumbs (figure 9).

Finally, a Scotch Brite pad is lightly rubbed along the rim to help expose the red earthenware beneath. This final touch helps create a little more depth to the surface once it has gone through the glaze firing. Note: For all three of the above steps that create crumbles or fine powder, wear a mask and work over a bucket of water to minimize the amount of dust entering the air and to make clean-up easier.

Glazing by Numbers

I bisque fire to cone 01, then, to prepare the piece for glazing, give it a good shower under running water to clean any leftover sgrafitto dust from the surface. Leave the piece to dry overnight. The first glaze application is like a paint-by-number painting. Often using two tones of the same color, I'll load up a small brush with the darker tone and fill in the "pod" shapes. Little pressure is used when painting as the glaze should flow from the brush onto the bisque, eliminating brush strokes (figure 10). I fill the sgrafitto lines with this first glaze, which helps eliminate pinholes in the glaze-fired impression. This first layer of glaze is left to dry several hours or even overnight.

The second, lighter tone of glaze is then poured on the plate in a similar fashion to the white slip—rotating a vertically-held plate clockwise while pouring the glaze in the middle of the piece (figure 11). This second coat is left to dry.

The final glazes are now ready to be applied to the dots using a small soft brush or a fingertip. I can usually see a light indentation of the sgrafitto dot through the poured glaze to use as a guide for dot placement. If I am unable to determine where to place my dot within the design, I sometimes guess and other times fire the piece and then apply the dots to the fired glaze and refire. The final dots are made up of a lighter-toned large dot with a smaller dark toned dot on top (figure 12).

The dry, glazed piece is fired to cone 04, held at that temperature for 15 minutes and then fired down to cone 010 before being turned off. This schedule helps to produce a nice satiny finish to the glaze surface.

Recipes

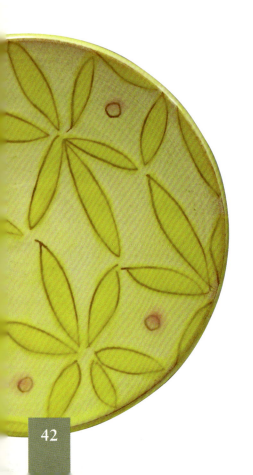

Pete's Forgiving White Slip
Cone 04

Talc	40 %
Nepheline Syenite	10
OM4 Ball Clay	40
Silica	10
	100 %

Can be applied to leather-hard, bone dry, or bisqued clay.

Satin Base
Cone 04

Ferro Frit 3124	65.5%
Nepheline Syenite	11.0
EPK Kaolin	5.5
Silica	18.0
	100.0%
Add: Bentonite	2.0

I use Mason stains to color this glaze. For the plate shown (right), the dark yellow is 4% MS Vanadium Yellow 6440, the light yellow is 2.5% praseodymium yellow 6450. Light and dark pinks are 1% and 2% MS Crimson 6003.

Add an Epsom salt solution to the wet glaze to help keep it suspended. Add the Epsom salts to boiling water until the solution is supersaturated. Add 1 tsp at a time until the glaze changes from thin and watery to light and fluffy, or the materials no longer settle out. Use 1 tsp for a 1000 gram batch and 3–4 tsp for a 5-gallon bucket.

Worthington Clear
Cone 04

Gerstley Borate	55 %
EPK Kaolin	30
Silica	15
	100 %

I use this base glaze along with colorants to create my red and orange glazes. (Used with 10% Degussa Orange stain for orange dots on the plates on page 17.)

Kat Red
Cone 04

Wollastonite	13.7%
Ferro Frit 3195	42.5
EPK Kaolin	23.5
Silica	10.7
	100.0%
Add: Bentonite	2.0
Degussa Bright Red stain	12.0

This is an opaque, fat-looking satin glaze. Used to make the dots on the plates on page 17.)

"Frosting" Maiolica
Cone 04

Ferro Frit 3195	54.8%
F4 Feldspar (Minspar 200)	14.3
Georgia Kaolin	4.5
EPK Kaolin	4.5
Nepheline Syenite	5.2
Zircopax	16.7
	100.0%

This glaze has the look of marshmallow when layered on top of my other glazes.

Layering Slips, Glazes and Decals

by Andrew Gilliatt

Identifying ways of working that successfully support your ideas can be just as critical and expressive as the ideas themselves.

With my functional pots, I'm designing pieces that, with the use of color and imagery, are expressive, visually inviting, and easily accessible for domestic use.

The process I developed includes sketching, using drafting software, making models with MDF, then making plaster molds from those models. The forms can then be repeated, and each one individualized through surface decoration and glazing.

Making Prototypes

Each new piece begins with a prototype, generally made of wood or MDF, from which I create a plaster mold. The prototypes can be made from clay, but I prefer using wood for its durability. I'm not the savviest mold maker, so if at some point I have an accident during the mold-making process, the prototype is safe and intact. I've also found that making prototypes from wood is great for achieving sharp, transitional lines and edges (figure 1). Once I've settled on a design, I produce two scale drawings—one illustrating the side view or profile, which includes the number of stacked pieces of MDF

Andrew Gilliatt's work combines colored porcelain slip, brightly colored glazes, resist patterns, and simple decals to create pots that convey the fun he has working in the studio.

1 Finished wooden prototypes of various vessels sealed with polyurethane.

2 Turn a solid, laminated MDF form on a lathe to get close to the right profile.

3 Finish shaping the prototype on a band saw and draw seam lines.

4 Add a clay slab to the sealed prototype to create a pouring gate or slip reservoir.

5 Pour colored casting slip into the plaster mold first.

6 Drain the excess colored casting slip from the plaster mold.

Reverse Shrinkage Equation

1 − shrinkage rate = X. Fired dimension of piece divided by X = prototype dimension.

For example:
My bowl needs to be 4 inches high when fired and my clay shrinks 16%
1 − .16 = .84
4 ÷ .84 = 4.76
My prototype needs to be 4.76 inches tall.

I will need to make the model, and one illustrating the top view. Using the first drawing as a blueprint, disks of MDF are cut, glued together, stacked, and turned on a lathe to make a solid round form whose shape is close to the side profile of the finished piece (figure 2). Tip: You can use a Surform tool to shape the MDF if you do not have a lathe. The second drawing works as a cutting template that is glued to the top of the form (see figure 2).

Using a band saw, I cut into the shape of the form, carefully following the outside edges of the glued-on template. The sides of the form are then sanded smooth to erase any irregularities from sawing. Finally, the prototype is sealed with one coat of Minwax Sanding Sealer and two coats of polyurethane.

The casting slip I use has a 16% shrinkage rate so the prototype must be made appropriately larger to accommodate the final size of the pot (see the reverse shrinkage equation for help with the math). Always test the shrinkage rate of your casting slip before making the prototype.

7 Cut away the pouring gate. Keep the blade flat on the top of the mold.

8 Finish the rim with a red rubber rib. Note the striations of contrasting colored slip.

9 Cast bowl, dried and ready to remove from the mold.

10 Decorate the bisqued bowl using masking tape and stickers.

11 Remove stickers and tape then clean up after the bowl has been dipped in glaze.

12 Applying the decal onto the fired bowl by sliding away the paper backing.

Making the Mold

When making molds, it's important to remember that casting, like any other building method, is strictly a means to a desired end. It doesn't have to be an overly technical venture and, depending on the form, can be quite easy. I've learned to make molds simply by reading books on the subject, and by asking for help from others.

The biggest trick to making molds is figuring out the number of parts to cast. Most of my molds are made with four parts—a bottom, two sides, and a top piece used as a pouring gate or slip reservoir. Before I make a mold, I take my prototype and draw seam lines on it with a black marker so that I know how many parts I will need for the mold (figure 3). Then I add a clay slab to the top of the prototype for a pouring gate (see figure 4). By making my pouring gate just a little taller than need be, I can control the quality of the rim after the piece has been cast.

Next, I embed the form into a block of clay up to the seam lines marking off the first section of the mold,

Recipes

Cone 10 Recipes "5,4,3,2,13" Porcelain Casting Slip

Grolleg	5 lb
Water	4 lb
Kona F4	3 lb
Silica	2 lb
	14 lb
Add: Sodium Silicate	13 g

Colored slip additions (Mason stains)

Black: MS 6600	100 g
Pink: MS 6020	120 g
Yellow: MS 6450	120 g
Blue: MS 6376	50 g
Orchid: MS 6332	25 g

14 pounds of slip is just under one gallon. To make colored casting slip, add 100–120 grams of commercial stain per one gallon of slip, then ball mill the slip for at least two hours to ensure even dispersal of the colorant.

Blue/Violet Glaze

Custer Feldspar	28.2 %
Wollastonite	26.5
Grolleg	20.7
Silica	24.6
	100.0 %
Add: Mason Stain 6332 Orchid	4.0 %

Translucent blue in reduction, purple in oxidation.

Green/Maroon Glaze

Strontium Carbonate	10 %
Cornwall Stone	40
Whiting	15
Grolleg	15
Silica	20
	100 %
Add: Mason Stain 6006 Deep Crimson	6 %

Translucent green in reduction, maroon in oxidation.

set up cottle boards, seal the seams between the blocking clay and the cottles, and pour the plaster. Parts of the blocking clay are removed as I'm ready to cast successive sections. The image shows the mold halfway through the casting process, with the bottom and first side cast, and the second side and slip reservoir or pouring gate still to be cast (figure 4). Note that the location of the seams has been planned so that they correspond to edges or places where planes and curves shift, rather than flat faces of the form. This makes them easier to clean up, and makes them less noticeable in the finished form.

Mixing the Casting Slip

Most of my pots are cast using two different slips—a colored casting slip for the exterior of the piece, and a white casting slip for the interior. Both are made from the same base recipe. The colored casting slips are tinted using Mason stains. Using only colored slip would be more expensive, and, lining the colored slip with a white slip allows me to get different color effects on the interior and exterior of a form using only one glaze.

The colored slip is essentially a decorative coating, much like an engobe applied to a thrown or handbuilt form, but in this case, the coating is laid down first.

To make the colored slip, ball mill 100 grams of stain per gallon of white casting slip and let them mix for two hours (14 lbs. of casting slip is roughly equivalent to one gallon). Ball milling gives a more consistent color saturation than blunging and the stain mixes in with the wet slip more easily. If you do not have a ball mill, use a kitchen blender and mix in small batches before combining.

Test shrinkage rates when using more than one slip in the same cast, even if they are made from the same base recipes. If the different slips have different rates of shrinkage, they will crack.

Casting the Pieces

Wet the mold with a sponge. Pour the colored casting slip into the mold and let it set up for approximately ten minutes (figure 5). Then pour the colored slip out of the mold and let it drain (figure 6). Once the slip has stopped dripping from the mold, immediately pour in the white casting slip. Leave the white slip in the mold for about 30 minutes before draining. The longer you leave the slip in the mold the thicker the piece will be. I prefer to make my pots just a little on the thicker side.

Finishing the Cast

Remove the top piece of the mold (here the pouring gate section is removed first) when the slip is no longer glossy or tacky. Using an X-Acto knife, cut away the excess clay. Hold the blade flush with the top of the mold as a guide, After piercing the form in one spot, angle the blade in the same direction of your cut so that you're always cutting the interior wall first, then moving through to the exterior. By doing so, you press the form back into the mold walls as you cut, and avoid warping the form by pulling the walls away from the mold (figure 7).

Smooth the rim with a damp sponge and a soft, flexible rib (figure 8). Let the piece dry sufficiently before removing it from the mold (figure 9). Once the piece is bone-dry, remove any seam lines with an X-Acto blade, fettling knife, or metal rib. Smooth away any inconsistencies using drywall sanding mesh and a sponge. Caution: Always wear a respirator when sanding pots.

Glazing and Firing

I leave patterned areas on the outside of my vessels unglazed to expose the colored clay underneath. Stickers and masking tape work great as a glaze resist and give a far crisper and better line quality than anything I can achieve using wax and a brush.

Clean the bisqued ware with a damp sponge. Using a pencil, outline the areas you want to leave bare. Follow the lines with masking tape (I use quarter-inch masking tape because it is more flexible than the wider tapes). For curved lines, focus on laying down just the outer edge of the tape rather than trying to lay down the whole width of the tape all at once (figure 10). With the resist pattern complete, dip or spray to apply the glaze. Peel away the tape and stickers as soon as the glaze is dry enough to handle (figure 11). Make sure to peel away the stickers entirely. Any remaining residue will leave a noticeable blemish even after firing.

Op Dot Jar, 7 in. (18 cm) in height, colored porcelain, glaze, fired to cone 10, decals added and fired to cone 2.

One upside to using different colored casting slips is that the glazes you use will have a different color quality on glazed and unglazed areas, depending on the color of the clay underneath, and the translucency of the glaze.

Laser Printer Decals

I make my own decals using a laser printer. I generate the images on a computer and then simply print onto water slide decal paper. HP laser printers work well and some types of copiers also make these decals. I use decal paper from www.papilio.com. You can also make handmade drawings to scale or use found images and then scan them into a computer or have them photocopied, just as long as they are printed on water slide decal paper. (For more information, you can also refer to the July 23, 2008 Ceramic Arts Daily feature "The Details on Decal Paper for Ceramics" by Paul Andrew Wandless.)

The iron oxide contained in the toner of laser printers is what makes this method work as a ceramic process. (This method will not work with ink jet printers!)

Laser printer decals work just like traditional water slide decals but with a few exceptions. For starters, the only color they fire to is a sepia or red ochre. Depending on what color clay or glaze you fire them on and depending on the opacity/transparency you select to print them, a broad range in tonality can be achieved. Secondly, these decals have no flux in them so they must be fired hotter than cone 018 (which is generally suitable for lusters, china paints, enamels, and overglazes) so that they melt to the glaze. I have found that cone 04–2 works best for high-fired ware.

For most glazed surfaces, you must fire the decals to at least cone 04. However, if your glazes are cone 04 the decals will dissolve away, so testing at a lower temperature is in order. For all of my cone 10 clay and glazes, I do a second decal firing to cone 2. At cone 2, the decals will fuse to both the glazed and unglazed areas. Any lower, the decals will melt only to the glazed surfaces.

Applying the Decals

After the glaze firing, sand any exposed areas of bare clay with 400-grit sandpaper for a smooth finish. Cut out the decal you wish to use. Don't worry about cutting away negative spaces, any excess material will burn away and this will make for easier application. Place the decal in room temperature water and wait for it to become fully saturated. Hold the decal onto the piece, ink side down, and slide away the paper (figure 12). The decals will still work if you don't place them ink side down, but the image may not be as clear.

With the decal placed on the ware, use a sponge or rubber rib to remove any excess water and to remove any air bubbles that might be trapped under the decal. Trapped air pockets may cause the image to bubble or become distorted. Be careful not to work the decals too hard; they are thin plastic and can tear easily. Make sure there is adequate lubrication when smoothing away air pockets. For large decals, or for decals that need to curve, use a hair dryer to lightly heat the decal to make it more pliable. Always let decals dry overnight before firing.

Elevating Earthenware

by Ben Carter

An interest in creating a sense of value through decoration, along with the ability of that decoration to craft meaning led me to work with earthenware. This might seem contradictory, since earthenware has common and utilitarian associations, but the choice is based very much on the history of the material.

The perceived value of earthenware has shifted throughout time. As a variety of techniques were explored, the level of decoration and experimentation increased. Major aesthetic breakthroughs occurred in the wake of the attempt to mimic porcelain. By covering earthenware with white slips or glazes, the objects also benefited from associations that porcelain had in the culture.

Making Templates and Molds

I begin by making a template in the shape and pattern of the rim of the platter, creating the template using tar-paper. Tarpaper can be used repeatedly because it's impervious to water. Cut the interior section of the template at both ends for easy registration on the form (figure 1).

Next, create a slump mold from stacked layers of closed-cell foam (the kind used for home insulation). The thickness of the mold depends on the depth of the recessed area required in the finished piece. I'd suggest making the mold at least 3 inches thick for strength. Mark the outline of the template onto the top of the stack. Individual sheets can be secured together using double

Dogwood Oval Platter, 20½ in. (52 cm), earthenware, painted slips, sgraffito, and glaze, fired to cone 3.

Create a tarpaper template of the platter. Make a stacked foam slump mold. Cut an opening in the foam 1½ inches in from the template's edge.

Use the tarpaper template to create a cloth mold that sits on the rim of the foam mold. Pin the cloth mold to the foam stack using T-pins.

Roll out a slab and trim it to the size of the tarpaper template. Place it so that the clay edge lines up with the edges of the cloth. Rib the slab into the mold.

Sandwich the removed oval section of blue foam, the cloth, and the platter (still in the slump mold) between your hands, then flip the piece.

sided tape. To create the recess in the slump mold, measure 1½ inches in toward the center from the two long ends and the two middle lobes of the outline and make a mark at each spot. Draw an oval connecting the dots, then use a serrated knife to cut out the shape.

Use the tarpaper template to aid in creating small cloth forms that sit on the rim of the foam mold (figure 2). The cloth forms are comprised of eight semi-circular sections that form a wavy rim for the platter. Make each cloth form using two pieces of canvas sewn together and filled with heavy grog. Pin the thinnest edge or point of the cloth form to the foam using T-pins (figure 3).

Making a Platter

Cut a 3/16-inch thick slab using the tarpaper template. Bevel or soften the edges of the slab and use a soft rubber rib to compress each side of the slab in both directions. Place the slab onto the stacked cloth and foam forms so that the slab edge lines up with the outside edges of the cloth form. Work the slab into the form

5 Be sure the rim sits parallel to and several inches above the table. Add a foot to the bottom of the piece and allow it to firm up.

6 Apply a white base coat of slip to the bottom and the rim. Apply a thick, colored slip to the interior using a soft bristle brush.

7 Sketch a design or motif onto the interior with a dull pencil. Press lightly so that you don't scratch through to the clay below.

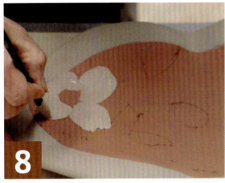

8 Brush lighter colore slips into the patterns. Use one coat for a translucent effect and multiple coats for more opacity.

9 Achieve a thicker sgraffito line on softer clay with a dull pencil, and a thinner, more detailed sgraffito line on harder clay with a needle tools.

using a soft rib and working both from end to end and side to side (figure 3). The advantage of this form is the ability to bend the slab on more than one axis, so take time to work the clay down into the curves.

Let the slab firm up to a leather-hard. Place a bundle of soft padding and the section of blue foam that was removed earlier into the platter's interior. Flip the whole stack over (figure 4). Make sure the rim rests parallel to your work surface and is elevated a few inches above it.

Extrude, handbuild, or throw a ring to form the foot. Curve the wall of the foot into a slight "C" shape with the curve flaring away from the center of the piece. Try to match the volume of the foot to the volume of the rim. Allow the foot to set up to the same leather-hard consistency as the piece before attaching it by slipping and scoring (figure 5).

Slipping and Sketching

After the foot has set up and can hold up the rest of the platter without slumping, flip it over and remove the padding and foam. Smooth out any marks made by the foam. Apply a base coat of white slip to the bottom and rim. Apply the slip by pouring it into smaller pieces and spraying larger ones. You can also paint the slip on using a brush. Allow the piece to dry between coats. Brush the interior surface of the form with colored slip, about the consistency of yogurt (figure 6). Note: When slipping greenware pieces, it's very important not to load the piece with too much moisture.

Once all the slip coats have dried, sketch a pattern or design onto the interior of the piece with a dull pencil (figure 7). Sketch lightly so the composition can be easily painted over if desired.

Brush colored slips, the consistency of pudding, into the drawn pattern (figure 8). Create gestural movement with your brush and the thicker slip by making quick direct strokes. Work from dark to light colors, allowing the dark slip to show behind the lighter slip and ultimately creating translucency and depth.

Use the sgraffito technique, scratching through the layers of slip to expose the clay body underneath. When fired, this dark line provides contrast to the lighter colored slips. If less contrast is desired, you may scratch through only the top layer of slip to expose the bottom layer. This line, whether high or low contrast, deep or shallow, works to sharpen the edges of the brush marks.

The timing of the sgraffito work affects the line quality. The moisture level of the clay should match the size of the tool. Start with the widest tools when the clay is a soft leather hard. As the pot dries, make finer lines with finer, sharper tools. For wide lines, use a chopstick sanded to a dull point. For small lines, use X-Acto blades and needle tools (figure 9).

Glazing

After decorating, allow the piece to dry slowly under a loosely wrapped layer of dry cleaner plastic. Dry larger pieces, like platters, for about a week before bisque firing. As the piece is drying, apply two coats of red terra sigillata to the foot to enhance the color and shine. For a deep maroon terra sigillata, add 1 tsp. of crocus martis per cup of liquid. Burnishing after each layer of terra sigillata helps create a lustrous shine.

Since pieces longer than twelve inches in any direction have a greater chance of cracking during the bisque fire, lightly sprinkle the kiln shelf with fine sand and place the piece on top of the sand. The sand acts as a shock absorber and allows for horizontal movement, reducing the stress on the platter. Allow ample space above the piece to promote even heat distribution, which helps avoid cracking in low, wide pieces.

After bisque firing, apply a transparent amber glaze over the interior of the platter. Apply a satin glaze to the rim and underside of the platter to provide contrast with the high gloss of the interior. Glaze fire the piece to the appropriate temperature for your glaze.

Forrest Lesch-Middelton
Layer by Layer

by Jeffrey Spahn

Five minaret bottles, to 18 in. (46 cm) in height, iron rich stoneware with iron transfer patterns, fired to cone 9, reduction-cooled.

Forrest Lesch-Middelton's pots evoke a similar response to what one gets from admiring sepia-toned photographs, antique embossed-tin roofing, or old press-typed announcements. They hark back to a different time in both their form and surface, yet they are made today with the aid of computers and silk-screened imagery. Each piece is timeless in feel, yet contemporary by design.

For some, this may seem like too much contrast, an aesthetic contradiction, but for Lesch-Middelton and his peers, the old and new, the complex and simple, mix easily with their world-view. Today's makers have been raised with interdisciplinary studies, multiculturalism, and access to every possible medium and process. Integration of complexity is the name of the game. Perhaps that is why Lesch-Middelton is so comfortable throwing and handbuilding, working with multiple firing atmospheres, or utilizing porcelain and stoneware. Traditionalists have their critiques for sure, no one discipline is deep enough, etc., but like it or not "mixing-it-up" is here to stay.

Lesch-Middelton's pots directly reference Islamic, Persian, Afghani and Iraqi forms and decoration. At the same time, his pottery is clearly made for a US market and for American ways of eating, drinking, and living. Lesch-Middelton's pots do not directly attack their viewer with overt messages about his opinions of the world, but rather they are subtle, beautiful pots that may, at times, encourage their owners to think deeply about where and when they were made, how and why they look the way they do, and what the maker himself is like. Lesch-Middelton summed up this feeling when he said, "I don't want the work I make to be about opinion, rather I would like it to be interesting enough to beg questions about me as a person with opinions who [also] makes pots." Lesch-Middelton has experienced many of these cultural contrasts in his own life. Raised from mixed cultural heritage, he saw

Above: Small dishes, 5¾ in. (15 cm) in diameter, iron rich stoneware with iron transfer patterns, fired to cone 9, reduction-cooled.

these contrasts directly. His mother is Native American, and works within indigenous communities on issues of cultural oppression and trauma, and his father is an architect and of mixed European decent.

Lesch-Middelton has been exaggerating the contrast in his work. Deep, rich, chocolate browns and blacks contrast with cream- and white-colored slips. Also, luscious forms and soft porcelains are embossed with textured surfaces and patterns. A simple sugar bowl and creamer become stacked forms, interlocking and with contrasting patterns. One, a traditional Texan calico pattern, is hoisted on top of a Middle-Eastern pattern, imperial style. Lesch-Middelton uses this to talk about his feelings when Bush invaded Iraq, and his need to make meaning of this. In this way he chooses to honor everyday functional pots, consistent with his daily values and philosophy of life. "My pots contain subtle narratives that reference the historic changes brought about when one culture's actions influence the course in which another culture proceeds," says Lesch-Middleton.

One of Lesch-Middelton's innovations comes with his slip and embossing techniques. Applied while the pieces are still wet and only partially formed on the wheel, the decoration morphs and changes as the form is shaped further during throwing, expanding and distorting as a reflection of the process. Pots are formed mostly from the inside out, as evidenced by the swelling and twisting of the exterior surfaces. He also throws in both forward and reverse directions to control the amount of torque and twist each piece achieves. Another innovation comes from the way Lesch-Middelton fires. He fires the pieces to temperature, then cools the kiln down in a reduction atmosphere, sometimes introducing localized oxidation at key points in the cooling.

The work shares similarities within the larger context of what's happening in contemporary crafts today. One observation is that makers today often seek decoration and embellishment. Perhaps it is because so much is already done today that the best makers spend their time and energy on decoration. Lesch-Middelton's work has its own aesthetic while sharing this focus on surface decoration with others such as Ayumi Horie, Kari Radasch, Jess Parker, Adam Field, Kristen Kieffer, and Ursula Hargens, to name a few.

Volumetric Image Transfer

by Forrest Lesch-Middelton

My work is planned layer-by-layer, both literally and figuratively. I start with an idea, a pot that to me has the feel of a weathered place prominent in my lifetime that has also stood the test of history. Once the layers and materials are chosen, the process begins with a pattern.

The patterns I use primarily come from the history of the Silk Road, which, to me, is a time and place in history that began to define the modern era. I fine-tune each pattern to a specific size and line density with the aid of Adobe Photoshop or Illustrator. By importing the image and adjusting color and contrast, I arrive at a black, photo-ready positive to be printed on a polyester laser transparency. The printed transparency is then laid over a light-sensitive photo silkscreen, exposed to light, and then washed out to create the final screen. When using ceramic materials as a screening medium, a 156-mesh screen is best. I order pre-exposed screens through a company in Vancouver, Washington, called Ryonet (www.ryonet.com). Send them an image, they send you a finished screen.

When printing with ceramic materials, it is important to use a printing medium compatible with the ceramic process. For colors, I use straight Crocus Martis, a naturally occurring 50/50 mix of black and red iron oxide, because it suits the very specific aesthetic needs of my work. You can use any ceramic oxide or stain.

The trick to my surfaces lies in transferring the image from the screen to the clay. For that you need a screening medium and some 25–30 pound newsprint. The recipe that I have found works best for a screening medium is a thick, white slip that is deflocculated to the consistency of sour cream. Deflocculating the slip allows it to become fluid with a smaller percentage of added water, which means it will not saturate or break down the newsprint when screened, and dries to a usable state more quickly. For color, add stain to the slip, mix it, and sieve through a 160-mesh screen. Next, add wet wallpaper paste (a starch-based glue that adheres the screened image to the newsprint) at a ratio of one-fifth the total volume of the slip. I have found that Roman's brand wallpaper paste for unpasted wallpaper works best because you can pour it straight from the jug into your screening medium. Once mixed, place a line or bead of the medium at the top of your screen and press it through onto a piece of newsprint using a printmaking squeegee. Once the image is on the paper, it only needs 20 minutes or so to dry and it is ready to use. When the transfer is re-wetted at a later time by painting a slip over the surface, it is able to stick to another surface (think temporary tattoo)!

In order to get each pattern to register around a thrown cylinder correctly, I have found junior high school geometry (like circumference = Π × diameter) comes in handy. First, tear or cut the pattern so that the pattern lines up correctly when wrapped end-to-end into a cylinder. Next, measure the length of the pattern with a metric ruler. This measurement will be the circumference of your cylinder. Once the image is measured, divide the total length by 3.14 and round down to get the diameter of the cylinder. For example: 33 cm/3.14=10.509, or 10.5 cm. Set your calipers to 10.5 cm and you are set to throw a cylinder. Each cylinder should be completely vertical and exactly 10.5 cm across.

Coat the freshly-thrown cylinder with the plain deflocculated slip using a hake brush. The deflocculated slip will dry more quickly, and will not add as much water to the form as a regular slip. This speeds up the drying process, allowing you to add the transfer sooner for more productivity. When the cylinder is coated evenly with

Screening slip ink onto the transfer newsprint.

Coating the image on newsprint with deflocculated slip.

the slip, coat the newsprint transfer on the side that contains the image. Once both surfaces are tacky to the touch, lift the newsprint off the table and stick it to the pot by wrapping it around the surface end to end, trying not to trap air bubbles (students say that this is the trickiest part). Use a flexible metal rib to adhere the newsprint gingerly to the cylinder with vertical strokes, starting at the bottom and moving upward. Once attached, peel off the newsprint and your image is transferred to the cylinder.

Once the image is in place it should not be touched or agitated in any way or it will smear. In order to add volume to the image-laden vertical form, you must belly the pot out from the interior. One issue that arose for me in working this way was the amount of torque that a wheel puts on the soft clay cylinder while it is spinning. To eliminate too much twisting, I carefully monitor the pattern while the pot spins, watching for twists. As a twist occurs in the pattern, I simply begin to spin the wheel in reverse and further belly out the form to counteract the distortion.

3 Carefully placing transfer newsprint around slip-coated cylinder.

4 Bellying out the cylinder to create a pitcher, stretching the pattern along with the form.

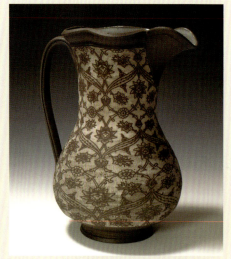

Large pitcher, 11¾ in. (30 cm) in height, iron rich stoneware with iron transfer pattern, fired to cone 9, reduction-cooled.

Blue and white cup, 4¾ in. (12 cm) in diameter, porcelain with cobalt transfer pattern, oxidation fired to cone 10.

Four cups, 4½ in. (11 cm) in height, iron rich stoneware with iron transfer patterns, fired to cone 9, reduction-cooled.

Paul Barchilon
Arabesque Designs

by Annie Chrietzberg

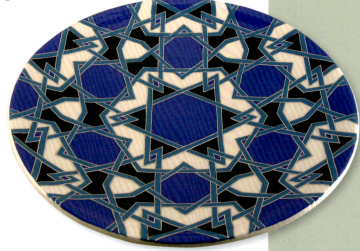

Enlightened Monarchs, 16 in. (41 cm) in diameter, glazed white earthenware with gold detailing.

Paul Barchilon's work is covered with complex and precisely laid out pattern. If you delve into his mind, you'll find that there is a structure and reason more complex and expansive than the work itself. Each one of his patterned pieces is an expression of a 1300 year old Islamic practice of creating pattern, called arabesque.

Paul's mother is a painter, his father was a professor of 17th-century French literature and is also of Moroccan heritage. During school holidays and for sabbaticals, Paul's family would go to Morocco to visit relatives, where Paul would spend extensive periods of time surrounded by architectural arabesque. He studied ceramics at the University of Colorado, Boulder, but left school early to give his full attention and exploration to observing and practicing arabesque patterns.

The arabesque motif, found in mosques and other forms of architecture, is an expression of the Islamic view of unity and the order of nature. Visually it relates to fractals (a rough or fragmented geometric shape that can be split into parts, each of which is, at least approximately, a reduced-size copy of the whole) but the pattern is ultimately done by the artist's hand and eye. Arabesque uses tessellation, which is the laying out of repeating shapes into patterns with no gaps or overlap to cover a surface or plane (think of MC Escher's work). In the geometric mode, which Paul uses, repeating shapes often have an integral symbolism, and the way these shapes tessellate in an infinitely expanding pattern relates to the underlying structure of the material world. This connection between the physical and spiritual nature of the world and art is known as sacred geometry in Western culture.

Generating a Pattern

First, determine the number of divided sections you want in your circle. The more divisions, the more complex your design can be. (See page 39 for tips on dividing a circle into six or twelve sections.) To make more or fewer divisions than what's shown, the same principles apply.

Here are the steps for drawing a complex pattern. Begin with a circle divided into fourteen equal parts.

Ceramic Arts Handbook

1

When creating designs, you have a couple of options. You can either sketch the idea on paper from start to finish (figure 1) or start with a sketch then create the pattern in Photoshop or Illustrator for greater control over the image and more flexibility to create variations on a theme (figures 2a–2f).

Once you have the circle drawn and divisions marked, you can choose to create the entire design on paper using a ruler and compass (figure 1), or scan in the drawing of the divided circle, open it in Photoshop or Illustrator, and continue working on the rest of the pattern on the computer (figures 2A–F). Since the pattern is repetitive, Paul finds that he reaches a point where it's more efficient to explore options with a design program. There are an infinite number of shapes that tessellate and it is easier to discover and

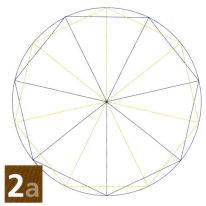

2a

Divide a circle into 14 equal parts. You can see two heptagons, one in blue and one in gold. In the final pattern, there will be two separate continuous lines that overlap each other just as these polygons do.

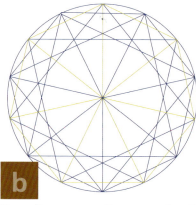

b

Draw lines connecting every fourth point to create a 14 pointed star inscribed within the heptagons.

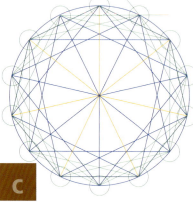

c

To create radial arms, draw circles around the periphery. These will be connected in the next stage. Next, connect every third point along the periphery. This will create intersections that define the actual pattern.

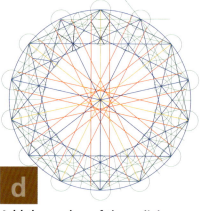

d

Add the spokes of the radial arms (in red) as well as a series of smaller circles whose intersections with other lines help define the shapes along the edge of the pattern.

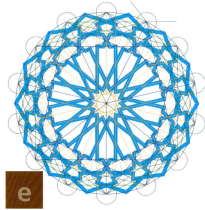

e

Draw thick lines that join all the intersections you want to use. If working on paper, start by making these lines in pencil then ink only the lines you want and erase the rest.

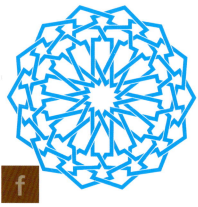

f

Erase the foundation lines and add in lighter outlines where lines intersect to create the interlace effect.

3
Trace the outlines of the pattern onto the platter using a pencil. Paul uses an opaque projector to display his paper patterns onto his work.

4
Start to build up the image with layers of slips or commercial underglazes. Start in the center and work your way out, painting the color in stages.

5
In between color stages, set the platter on a drafting table. The rope loops around the foot ring and holds the platter in place.

6
Articulate and sharpen the lines with a carving tool and remove any debris with a soft brush.

7
With each new layer, the pattern expands. The refined edges of various shapes are visible as lightly carved lines.

8
For all designs, alternate between building up the color layers and refining the lines of the pattern.

to manipulate the pattern digitally. Exploring possible color schemes is easier to do digitally as well.

Regardless of whether you work on paper or on a computer, each step builds a layer of lines and circles based on the first set of divisions you made. In figure 2A, you can see two heptagons, one in blue and one in gold. In the final pattern, there will be two separate continuous lines that overlap each other the same way these two polygons do. Next, draw lines connecting every fourth point. This creates a 14 pointed star which is inscribed within the heptagons (figure 2B).

9
Starlight, 16 in. (41 cm) in diameter, glazed earthenware, by Paul Barchilon.

To add parallel, spoke-like lines that radiate from either side of the exact center point of the design, draw circles around each point along the perimeter. They will delineate the spacing between the pairs of radiating spokes (see the red lines in figure 2D). Connect every third point along the periphery; these lines will create intersections needed to create the actual pattern (figure 2C). Draw in the spokes of the greater arms (in red) as well as a series of smaller circles whose intersections with other lines help define the shapes along the edge of the pattern (figure 2D).

Draw thick lines that join all the intersections you want to use (figure 2E). This step takes a very long time to do in pencil and ink on paper, and requires a lot of guidelines to be drawn in. Using a computer, this step can be completed in just a few hours. Finally, hide all the layers with foundation lines (in Photoshop) and add in small white lines to create the interlace effect (figure 2F). This process takes about 30 hours of designing, drawing, and then completing the pattern on the computer.

Transferring and Painting the Pattern

When the pattern is finished, print it out and use an overhead opaque projector to project the image onto an unfired platter. Carefully trace each shape with a pencil or sharp tool (figure 3). Wipe away any excess debris with a soft brush and then begin to apply commercial slips or underglazes (Paul uses Duncan Cover Coat and Amaco Velvet Underglazes) to build up the pattern in color stages (figure 4). Paul recommends sitting in a slightly reclined position and using large pieces of foam to support the work comfortably in your lap. In between each color layer application, move the piece to a drafting table (figure 5) and use a sharp tool to refine the edges and lines (figures 6 & 7). Alternate stages of decoration between applying color and carving the patterns lines to sharpen them and clean up the edges. The articulating of each line removes any messy painting lines (figure 8). This alternating process of painting and refinement allows for a high level of detail in the finished piece (figure 9).

Paul uses two commercial clay bodies—red and white, purely for aesthetic reasons. He lets the color of the clay show through and it becomes part of the pattern. He bisque fires after painting the patterns, then applies a clear glaze and fires again. He occasionally uses gold luster on the glazed ware and fires a third time.

Designing for Food

by Gwendolyn Yoppolo

The design of food preparation tools involves more than ergonomics. The pieces we create shape our full physical and metaphysical interaction with the world, and are embedded within a larger cultural system of values. My vision for our future with food involves people working with whole foods in a direct way to craft their own nourishment, so I've been developing a line of kitchen tools with that goal. These include mortars and pestles, sieves, spooning utensils, graters, and juicers.

Design Considerations

In designing a juicer form, you've got a few decisions to consider. The first is the specific purpose of the juicer—will it juice small citrus (lemons and limes) or larger citrus (oranges and grapefruits)?

With the juicer and bowl form here, the juicer form, which is the site of reaming action, hangs over a receiving bowl that's also a pouring form. The three purposes—reaming, catching, and offering—must be integrated into an overall form that's stable during the juicing but not too heavy during the pouring.

Another consideration involves the straining of the pulp and/or seeds from the juice. You'll have to decide how much pulp you want in your juice, and design a straining mechanism that catches the seeds but allows the desired amount of pulp through. Start your process with a strong idea for how to answer these design issues, then sketch profile and cut-away views of the form, inside and out. For the purposes here, when I refer to the bowl I am talking about the lower receiving bowl; when I refer to the juicer I am talking about the hanging reamer section.

Expand your concept of whole foods to include aesthetic nourishment, as in this two part juicer by gwendolyn yoppolo made from thrown and hand-built porcelain with microcrystalline glazes, and fired to cone 10 in an electric kiln.

Measuring inside diameter of the rim of the freshly thrown bowl.

Measuring the diameter of the juicer to ensure proper fit.

Compressing the clay after trimming the juicer bottom.

Forming the handle for the bowl.

Wet Forming Phase

First, in the wet forming phase, throw a bowl and measure the inside rim (figure 1). The juicer hangs inside this rim, so the inside diameter is the important measurement.

Next, throw the juicer. It's shaped like a shallow bowl or low plate (figure 2), depending on how you would like it to curve over or into the bowl. When throwing the juicer, remember that the outer edge of the juicer rim will be trimmed down to an oval shape to match the hand-built handle added to the bowl, so be sure to be generous with the amount of clay you leave for the overhang. Be sure to leave enough width between the rim and center of the juicer for the fingers and orange to rotate around the reaming area.

As you'll see below, I have a separate mold that I use to make the reamer, which I make later. I estimate the diameter of the juicer based on this mold.

Soft Altering and Building

When the parts are set up just enough (soft leather hard), you can trim the juicer on the wheel (figure 3). You'll trim and shape the bowl using a rasp later, so that you can create an oval foot. Since the juicer is designed to fit inside of the round rim of the bowl, the bottom can be trimmed on the wheel so that it registers properly when placed on the bowl. The juicer rim will be re-

5 Use a paper pattern to determine the size and shape of the spout.

6 Compressing the clay while attaching the handle to the bowl.

7 Perforations cut into the wall of the bowl leading into the spout.

8 The reamer freshly popped off of the mold.

shaped later to fit the curve of the bowl's rim, so after trimming, moisten the edge and wrap it in a strip of plastic several times.

Shape the spout and handle for the bowl. The handle can be built from slabs, coils, or a solid form that's hollowed out later. I prefer the solid form technique, because it allows the handle to be shaped into a unified form with the bowl once finished (figure 4). Pinch the handle into a rough shape, then let it stiffen to a soft cheese consistency before hollowing it out.

While the handle dries, work on the spout. Use a quick paper pattern to estimate the shape of the slab needed to attach to the front of the bowl (figure 5). Reshape the slab slightly to give it a more generous pouring throat, then attach it to the front of the bowl, working the joint together with metal ribs so that the spout and bowl form flow together. You might want to add a coil on the inside of the spout to round the edge and guard against cracking.

When the bowl handle has stiffened, hollow it out from the inside so the walls are an even thickness, then attach it to the bowl using a basic slip and score method and pressure from a metal rib (figure 6). Shape the rib to achieve an upward movement that continues the curve of the bowl. Be sure to create a hole in an inconspicuous place on the

9 Adding a handle to the juicer.

10 Attaching the foot to a slab to create a hollow foot.

11 Using drills to mark off areas to remove for seed-catching slots.

12 Cutting the seed-catching slots using a utility knife.

13 Using a loop tool to soften the edges of the perforations in the spout area.

handle so that air can escape as it expands during the firing, otherwise the piece may explode. At this point, cut or drill perforations in the wall of the bowl leading to the spout, or cut this part of the wall out completely (figure 7). Even if you decide not to have a perforated wall in this part of the bowl, it's good to leave the upper rim whole, since the juicer will hang there and could use the support. Allow the bowl to set up slowly while you work on the juicer.

Now mold the reamer cone using a plaster or bisqued slump or hump mold. The reamer mold can be made from a commercial juicer or your own design. Drape a slab into or over the mold, using a sponge to work it into the crevices and over the protrusions. After sponging the form, I sharpen the edges with a rubber rib. The slab dries quickly and can be separated from the mold within a few minutes (figure 8).

Before joining the reamer cone to the juicer, reshape the juicer to fit to the rim of the bowl. If you need to wrap the reamer until the juicer is ready, do so. The two parts should be of similar dryness when joined.

Uniting the Parts

Place the juicer on the bowl, working it gradually onto the bowl's curved rim with a sponge. The spout and the handle additions have created a flowing curve for the juicer to follow. Work the edges of the juicer so that they hang over the rim of the bowl, this will keep the juicer from sliding around too much during use. After sponging the rim to get the contour, use a metal or rubber rib on that area to compress, form, or shape the clay.

Attach the reamer to the juicer, adding a small coil of clay around the base to guard against cracking. Remove the part of the juicer bottom underneath the reamer to expose the interior. Make sure the juicer is not bending as you work. Also, don't worry too much now about clarifying the lines under there—it's better to wait until the juicer has set up to a harder cheese consistency to clean it up. If you'd rather leave the bottom of the juicer intact, that's fine, but remember to poke a small air hole in the bottom like the one made in the handle.

The juicer in action: gwendolyn yoppolo thinks a lot about whole foods and the pots she designs to make preparing these foods a part of people's everyday lives.

Place the juicer on the rim of the bowl after wrapping the bowl rim in plastic to keep the two separate. Attach clay on the handle end of the juicer so that it matches the bowl's handle and provides the person juicing with a good grip on both of them (figure 9).

This is a good time to wrap any part that seems to be drying too fast (like the rim of the bowl) with plastic, then wrap the entire pot in plastic and let it sit, at least overnight. Such periods of rest within an airtight environment allow for even moisture redistribution within the piece.

Remove, Reduce, Refine

For the next phase, which involves trimming the bowl and perforating the juicer, the piece should be leather hard. To trim the foot on the bowl, use a rasp to remove clay, creating an oval form for the foot of the bowl that responds to the oval form created by the spout and handle. After rasping away the clay on the outside of the foot, remove the clay from the interior of the foot using a small loop tool. This can be left as an open foot ring, but I like to cover the foot ring with a slab of clay, creating another hollow area on the bowl (figure 10). This requires an air hole on the bottom of the pot like the one made in the handle.

Reassemble the juicer and bowl, and use the rasp to remove excess clay on the juicer rim. Sharpen and clean up the edge on the underside of the juicer around the inverted reamer. Next, carve out perforations that will allow juice and pulp to fall into the bowl, while catching seeds. Drill small holes encircling the base of the reamer, following its contour and slightly larger holes toward the rim of the juicer (figure 11). Use a utility knife to join the holes, cutting slots that encircle the reamer (figure 12). Again, at this stage, wrap the pot and allow it to rest.

The next phase is one of refinement and reduction. When the pot is almost bone dry, gently scrape away unwanted marks and excess clay using metal ribs and loop tools. The purpose of this almost-dry trimming might be to lighten the bowl, to remove unwanted rasp marks, to cut a sharper foot ring, to clarify a curve, or to soften an edge. Sharp curved tools or small loop tools are handy for trimming the edges of the perforations in the spout wall (figure 13). I like those edges to be soft to correspond to the manner of the other edges in the piece. The holes in the juicer can be refined using a pin tool. Now the forms can be air-dried, with perhaps a light covering of plastic if your room isn't very humid.

Finally, when the pot is bone dry, use a sponge to erode away any unwanted marks or slight inconsistencies. A cosmetic sponge or a paintbrush works well to soften the edges of the perforated slots. Sponging a bone dry form is also nice because it reduces the amount of sanding that needs to be done before or after bisque firing.

Glazing Considerations

When glazing this form, remember that these two forms need to be fired together to ensure a proper fit after the firing. This means that the entire top surface of the bowl's rim will be unglazed, as will the underside of the juicer rim. You can use a coil of wadding to separate the parts during the firing if you're worried about them fusing together at all. I use a liner glaze inside the bowl and inside the juicer, and matt microcrystalline glazes on the exterior of the bowl and on the rim of the juicer. Once the pot is fired, I use wet silicon carbide sandpaper to polish any areas of raw porcelain. This leaves all areas of the pot feeling very soft to the touch.

Making Bisque Molds

by Nancy Zoller

The way that clay stamps can activate and transform the clay surface has been a constant source of fascination to me, helping my work evolve and grow over the last three decades. I've worked with traditional, impressed designs, and more recently with raised designs created via a two-step process.

The platters with raised patterns are created using a hump mold and slab construction. First a pattern is stamped into a slab that's been draped over a form, then this slab is dried and bisqued to create the mold.

The surface designs on the mold create a convex, or raised pattern rather than the typical concave surface achieved with stamps. I came up with this idea a few years ago after becoming frustrated with the way traditional stamped patterns did not hold up when using drape molds. I wanted to make utilitarian forms that were elegant, had fine detail and could be reproduced. It was also essential to me that making these pieces kept my joy for working with clay alive!

Finding Mold Forms

There are never-ending sources of forms all around us to use as base shapes. Plastic or metal mixing bowls and even a solid centered mound of clay shaped into a low, gradually curved form and dried to the leather-hard state will work.

The form must function as an exterior drape or hump mold. If you find an interior shape you like, simply make a plaster mold using #1 Pottery Plaster. Be sure to spray the interior of the form with cooking spray or coat with Vaseline or A&D ointment as a release agent, then pour the plaster inside the form. Remember that plaster expands slightly as it hardens, so it's best to avoid making a mold of anything too fragile.

To make large platter molds, I first create a plaster mold using a Slump Hump form, which is a plastic mold form that can create both slump molds and hump molds. Slump-Hump forms are available in a variety of shapes and sizes at ceramic supply companies.

Round convex maple leaf platter, 13 in. (33 cm) in diameter. Photo credit: Jafe Parsons.

1 Lay a ¼-inch slab over the exterior drape mold and trim the excess following the base of the form.

2 Stamp into the form, using handmade bisque or plaster stamps or found objects.

3 Add a throwing spiral with a metal rib and create emphasis with a small leaf stamp. Dry and bisque fire.

4 Drape a ¼-inch thick slab over the bisque-fired mold and trim the excess following the rim.

5 Firmly roll a small hand roller from the center of the slab to the outside edge. Cut at the base of the form.

6 Center the mold on the wheel, make marks for the foot ring and extrude a ½-inch coil for the foot.

Making the Bisque Mold

Once you've found or made a drape form, you're ready to start making your bisque mold on top of it. Roll out a slab of clay about ¼-inch thick and place it over your drape mold (figure 1). If your drape form is glass or metal, place a piece of plastic wrap between the form and the clay to keep the slab from sticking. Cut and smooth the bottom edge so that it's a straight, even and level line, following the base of the form.

Stamp into the clay surface as if you were making a piece with a concave, design (figure 2). Make your own clay stamps or use items from nature such as shells, pine cones, and leaves. Using a wheel and a ribbon or loop tool, carve borders or defining lines to frame in your design. Remember that whatever is carved into the clay will be raised and reversed in your future piece.

If the mold is round, place it on the wheel, center it and secure it with lugs of clay as you would when trimming and use a metal rib to create a spiral in the middle giving it a "thrown" appearance if you wish. Usually, a small leaf finds its way

7 Press down on the inside and outside to attach the coil, then pull up to create the foot. Smooth with a sponge.

8 For a square piece, attach a coil foot and smooth the inside transition with a rubber rib.

9 Stamp the outside of the coil with stamps similar to the shape on the mold to create continuity.

10 Carve the edge of platter with a fettling knife to accentuate the stamped motif.

into the interior of the design on my work (figure 3). Once you've finished the design work, wait until the piece is leather hard and remove it from the mold. Let the form dry slowly, then bisque fire it.

Final Convex Piece

Roll out a slab of clay and place it over the bisque mold (figure 4). With a small hand roller firmly roll the clay from the center of the mold out toward the edge (figure 5). Use a rubber rib to smooth this surface after rolling. Cut and smooth the bottom edge with a needle tool following the base of the mold.

At this point, you can extrude a ½-inch thick coil to add a raised foot to the form. The clay and the coil need to be the same wetness. If the form is round, place the mold on the wheel, center it, and secure it with clay lugs, and throw the foot. Using your pin tool, make two concentric circles about a half inch apart while the wheel is spinning to indicate where you will place the coil. Place the coil (figure 6), then press downward on the inside and outside of it to adhere it to the base surface. Once it's fastened, firmly give the coil an upward pull to create height, then smooth the surface with a chamois or sponge (figure 7).

To add the coil to an oval, square or oblong form, simply eyeball where you want it. Lay the coil down and be sure to bevel the edges where they join to secure the connection. Use a flat wooden tool to smooth the coil on the inside creating a secure join. When the coil is secured, smooth the transition between the coil and pot with a rubber rib (figure 8). Use similar clay stamps on the outside of the foot to tie the patterns together (figure 9).

Revealing the Finished Piece

Clay dries and releases very quickly on a bisque-fired mold, which allows for several pieces to be made on the same mold each day.

When the platter is leather hard, pop it off of the mold. At this point, clean up the outer edge with a fettling knife. The outer edge can be a straight line or follow the contours of the stamped shapes (figure 10). After cutting, smooth the edge with a sponge. I sometimes add slip-trailed elements or do more carving on the surface of the piece. Adding handles to larger pieces enhances the form and makes them easier to use. Since you've already added a foot, the piece is now complete.

Glazing

Semi-matte, shiny, or transparent glazes work best in highlighting the raised surface design on these pieces. I use one glaze on the whole piece, then brush another accent glaze or stain onto the leaves, shells, etc. Spraying or dipping the piece all at one time with no glaze overlapping is best, as overlaps create lines that will distract from the raised pattern.

Final Thoughts

Creating and using these molds offers me endless possibilities. As a pottery instructor, it assures quick success for the most novice of my clay students. In addition to helping beginners, this technique presents an excellent road into exploration when used by seasoned clay artists as well.

Marcos Lewis
Urchin Texture

by Annie Chrietzberg

Large urchin form made from dark brown stoneware and porcelain slip, glazed with a green celadon; two smaller urchin forms, both made from porcelain and porcelain slip, one with a pale blue celadon, and the other with a clear glaze.

Surface Glaze&Form

Marcos Lewis' Sea Urchin vessels are inspired by the time when he lived in the Pacific Northwest working as a commercial fisherman. "All my years, first as a kid on the beach digging clams, looking under rocks, and later working as a commercial fisherman, have filled my memory with shapes and patterns," he states. Marcos has been making sea urchin forms for about seven years and he has developed a process and a few tricks along the way that he's happy to share.

Marcos throws his urchin form on the wheel, using a rib to form the inside, then closes the form until only a tiny hole remains on top (figure 1). He throws with very little water in order to trim and decorate as quickly as possible. Once the piece has set up to leather hard, he places the pot back on the wheel and brushes the inside of it with a white slip. He then trims the outside of the form to match the space he created on the inside, taking care to leave an even wall (figure 2).

After trimming, Marcos uses a ball syringe with a piece of an ink tube from a ballpoint pen fitted into the end to slip trail the textured bumps similar to a sea urchin. As he trails slip, he scores the surface of the pot with the tip of the ball syringe for better adhesion (figure 3). "When making the beads of slip, I tend to poke and jab the plastic tip of my trailer into the clay, this makes small cuts and dents in the clay under the slip and gives the slip a rough scratched surface to adhere to. I also sometimes go back and gently press the bumps onto the clay as they dry if I see some

1

Throw the urchin form by bellying out then collaring in a cylinder and close it leaving only a small opening.

2

Place the piece upside-down in a padded chuck and then trim the bottom.

3

Slip trail a pattern of dots. Use the end the slip trailer to score the piece as you apply the slip.

separation happening," he notes. When his syringe is not in use, he uses a piece of guitar string to plug the hole. He joked, "It's ironic that when I was a commercial fisherman in Alaska, I used to keep my hands in shape when not fishing by squeezing a rubber ball, now I make my living by squeezing a rubber ball!"

Laying out the patterns by eye, Marcos makes a first line of bumps from the top of the pot, straight down the side of the pot, then does the next line directly opposite the first. By eye he finds the halfway point between two existing lines and continues his decoration around the pot, but he doesn't always stick to straight lines. He's made a special tool to clean up around the bumps if he needs to; he simply ripped the foam rubber off of a disposable paint brush, and cut the plastic support inside down to the exact shape and size he needs. "This is also a good tool for cleaning up around handles," he said (figure 4).

Marcos is experimental with his clay bodies, slips, and firing meth-

4

Left to right: A disposable paint brush handle with the plastic support trimmed down, a wooden rib, and a squeeze bulb with a piece of an ink tube and a guitar string.

ods. He'll run the gamut from using a white porcelain slip on a dark clay body and creating an atmospheric effect with soda ash, to a stark white on white with a clear glaze, and everything in between. He'll even modify the density of bumps to get particular effects from 'stunt glazing'. "I pretty much use any combination [of clay, slip, and firing] I can get my hands on, low fire, micaceous, standard high fire, reduction, salt, soda, etc. If there is any combination that I haven't tried yet, then I plan on it!"

Etched in Clay

by Jim Gottuso

A water abraded surface of calligraphic lines decorates the surface of Jim Gottuso's clean-lined forms.

A few years ago, I developed an interest in trying to exploit the use of wax resist in the service of surface decoration. I was disappointed with the waxes I tried on both bisqueware and greenware. They were globs of goo that didn't respond to thin brushes or delicate application.

At the same time I happened upon the work of Arne Ase whose work absolutely floored me, especially after unsuccessfully trying wax, paraffin, and acrylic medium on greenware in an attempt to etch the unprotected areas and create depth to the surface. His decorations were incredibly delicate and, of course, his use of soluble salts and translucent porcelain came together in pieces of sublime beauty. What wasn't clear was what he used for a resist. It turns out that Arne had written *Water Colour On Porcelain,* which has been described as the definitive book on soluble salt use and the secret ingredient had to be in that book. Unfortunately it is out of print, but the library managed to find a copy, and the book revealed the ingredient as shellac.

Fellow blogger, Michael Kline, says that at Penland the process of using a resist and dissolving the exposed unfired clay was referred to as "hydro-abrasion". After a couple of years trial-and-error and evolving a personal visual vocabulary, it turns out that this process dovetails very nicely with what appeals to my sense of design, form, and aesthetics. I've always loved what happens when a brush, pen or pencil makes contact with another surface, and using shellac as a resist on dried, unfired clay allows the surface to be etched without losing the immediacy and spontaneity of such brushwork.

Materials

For this technique, you will need shellac, denatured alcohol, brush, sponge, water, and an OSHA approved respirator.

Shellac thickens when exposed to air and loses its ability to soak into the clay body thoroughly. It can be thinned with alcohol, but over time it loses its viscosity and eventually needs to be discarded. Avoid the waste by decanting only what you need into a small lidded jar.

1. Apply resist to both the foot and rim to preserve their integrity throughout the process.

2. Apply the first (and ultimately foreground) layer of resist for your chosen design.

3. Allow the shellac to completely dry and remove clay from the exposed areas using a damp sponge.

4. Apply shellac over the top of the first layer, making this second layer extend about 1/8 inch past the edge.

5. Brush shellac in the remaining un-protected areas, leaving only a small gap between the two covered areas.

Thinking in Reverse

Begin with a bone dry, trimmed piece. Since my pieces are typically about ¼-inch thick, tapering to 3/16-inch at the rim, I'm careful not to put a strain on it. This process requires a bit of thinking in reverse. Protect the parts of the piece that are not to be altered. The first layer of shellac resist applied to the piece, because it covers the clay before any abrasion takes place, ends up being the topmost layer, or highest relief area at the end of the process. Since I don't want the rim or foot to be etched, I apply resist to both to preserve their integrity (figure 1).

Defining the Foreground

The next step is to apply the first layer of resist that creates the decoration and results in the top or foreground layer of the final design (figure 2). Imagine writing your name with the shellac then etching the un-shellacked areas. If, after that another layer of shellac was applied in a grid pattern over the name and etched again, the result would appear as your name hovering over the grid, even though the applications were done in reverse. For the finished piece here, the first layer is a series of vertical calligraphic marks that go from the foot to the rim.

6 Allow the piece to dry again and repeat the etching process. Continue these steps until you are satisfied.

7 Brush a black slip that is suitable for use on greenware over the entire surface of the outside of the bowl.

8 Use a sponge to wipe off any black slip that is not in the etched lines.

9 Go over the entire surface with a stiff brush after the bisque firing to clean off the shellac residue.

Abrading the Clay

Allow the shellac to dry completely (24 hours), then start abrading the exposed areas with a damp sponge (figure 3). If you intend to preserve what's been laid down in shellac without degradation, jettison the idea of abrasion, and think of your goal in the process as more like dissolving the clay, even though that's not technically what's happening.

Abrasion occurs when the water between the sponge and the surface collects dislodged clay particles in it and creates a localized slurry, which gets thicker and thicker as you go. Do not leave this thick slurry between the sponge and the pot. When the sponge has lots of clay on the surface and little water left in it, you're likely to eradicate your image along with the unprotected areas as the particles on the sponge move across and scratch into the surface.

To avoid this, load a sponge with water and wipe the surface of the pot until the slurry starts to form, then rinse the sponge thoroughly in your bucket of water and repeat. In this early stage, with large unprotected areas of clay, this means you're having to rinse out the sponge frequently, sometimes after only two swipes across the clay.

Defining the Middle Ground

After allowing the piece to completely dry again apply a second layer of shellac. I'm trying to create the appearance on the final bowl of a thin brush stroke that's hovering or sitting on top of another, slightly wider, brush stroke. I apply shellac over the top of the original shellac lines and make this second layer extend about ⅛ inch past the edge of that first layer (figure 4).

Adding Linear Elements

On this particular bowl, my goal is to have a linear reinforcement of the negative space that's created by the slightly widening brushwork. To achieve this, apply shellac in all the remaining unprotected areas, leaving only a small (⅛–³⁄₁₆ inch) gap of bare clay between the two covered areas (figure 5).

Allow the piece to dry and repeat the etching process (figure 6). When you notice a slurry developing, rinse the sponge to avoid abrading the edges of the resisted areas, otherwise your lines may have jagged rather than crisp edges. Since the area being dissolved now is linear as opposed to large planes, moving in a circular motion with the sponge aids in getting a uniform depth to the etching. It can be particularly difficult to gauge how deep the etching is now because the layers of shellac have some thickness or depth themselves. The shellac will eventually burn out in the bisque and only then is the depth and uniformity of the etching revealed.

Adding Color

Let the piece dry completely then brush on a black slip over the entire exterior of the bowl (figure 7). My black slip is made from throwing slip reclaim and 35 grams of Mason stain #6600 black added per 2 cups of slip.

Wipe off any slip that is not in between the etched lines before it dries (figure 8). If you accidentally take too much slip off and there are unprotected areas that are now back to bare clay, it's easy to reapply more slip immediately to that area and try again allow it to dry.

Glazing Strategies

When the bowl is bisque fired, you'll finally be able to see how the decoration looks, from the subtleties of the etched layers to the contrast between the dark and light tones of the slipped and bare areas. If a flaky residue is present from the shellac, brush the entire surface with a stiff brush to clean it up (figure 9) or it will wreak havoc.

When glazing, I dip my pots but spraying, pouring and painting the glaze also works. Of course, in order to accentuate the subtle differences in relief, transparent or translucent glazes, or glazes that break over texture and edges, works the best. If the colored slip is dark (like this black one), a darker glaze cuts way down on the contrast. Note: Since the relief is low, a thin glaze application works better since a thicker glaze on the finished piece will soften the etched effect.

Glaze Etching

by Ann Ruel

Etching cream can embellish the glaze surface in the same way it is used with glassware.

Using etching cream to embellish glassware is a favorite technique among DIY crafters. Etching cream is an acidic liquid that attacks the glass surface, creating matte areas. Of course, since fired glazes are a form of glass, it would make sense that many of them will react to the chemicals in etching cream as well.

Inspired by Sabra Wood, a potter from Crocus Clay Works in Rochester, New York, I did a little experimenting with etching cream to create matte patterns on finished, glaze-fired surfaces. I took a sampling of some of the glazed test tiles I had available in my studio and etched a design onto them.

On each of the tiles, the etched design appeared, but the most successful tests with the most prominent patterns were those where the surface of the glaze was both glossy and opaque. On these tiles, the area covered with the etching cream resulted in a matte surface, which really stood out against the shiny background.

Etching cream can be found in craft stores and is fairly easy to use. It contains harmful ammonium/sodium biflourides and needs to be handled carefully. You must read the label of the product that you purchase and follow the safety warnings. Be careful not to etch surfaces that will come in contact with food.

1. Draw the design onto the tape and cut away the positive areas.

2. Generously apply the etching cream ONLY to the areas to be etched.

3. After approximately 1–5 minutes, rinse away the etching cream.

The etching cream deteriorates the finish on your glazed surface. It is possible that the etchings may leave these areas susceptible to further breakdown from acidic substances it may come in contact with.

Matte on Shiny

Etching cream is very thick and can easily be applied to a glaze surface with a paint brush. Because the cream is thick, it's less likely to run or move and thus can be manipulated on vertical or horizontal pottery pieces. For example, Sabra prefers to apply the cream over the entire surface of her sculptures so the high areas become etched while recesses retain their original glazed character.

The technique I prefer is to apply the cream to create individual motifs. Achieving intricate, hard-edged designs can be difficult due to the viscous nature of the chemical, so I came up with techniques for applying the chemical freehanded.

One technique is to apply the cream using simple stamps or into lines that were carved into the clay while it was leather hard. After the glaze firing, these I also apply the cream using a masked-off surface and/or using stencils. Craft stores sell contact vinyl, which easily adheres to a clean glaze surface and can be used to create stencils. As an alternative, and less expensive method, I substitute masking tape for the vinyl. It's just as easy to trace designs onto the tape and then cut out the positive areas with an X-Acto blade as it is on the vinyl. Just be sure that the tape is pressed firmly onto the glazed surface.

Once the pattern is cut, remove the excess tape to reveal the visible areas (figure 1). Make sure that the tape is securely adhered, especially along the edges. Apply a thick and even coating of the etching cream to the exposed areas (figure 2). Note: The cream will etch whatever it touches so be sure you only apply it only to areas you intend to etch.

After a few minutes, wash the cream off with running water (figure 3) and peel off the stencil or masking tape. Dry the area thoroughly with a paper towel to reveal your design.

Surface
Glaze&Form

A Rainbow Revealed

by Adrian Sandstrom

One of my most memorable art assignments as a kid was to scribble multiple colors with crayons onto a sheet of paper and once it was completed, to paint over it completely with black tempera paint so that all of that color was hidden from view. When the paint dried, we used a paper clip and scratched through the black surface, revealing lines of brilliant color. I was completely fascinated with how all of the colors came through, and continued to draw circle after circle, until I had basically uncovered all of my original colors.

I have always had a simple love of the circular shape and have doodled imperfect and perfect circles for as long as I can remember. Once I was introduced to ceramics, it only made sense that I would start to incorporate the circle into my work, as well as relive my favorite childhood art project. The first time I tried it, I added the circles to the piece with slip onto a greenware piece. After numerous attempts, I discovered that by adding slip over underglazes and then carving the circles into the slip, the piece had a much more dramatic look in which the circles appeared to be floating on the pot. I've just scratched (no pun intended) the surface with this technique and look forward to how it evolves over time.

Applying Color

To start, take a bisqueware piece and make sure it's completely dry and free of dust. I chose to use bisque ware instead of greenware because I work on a fairly large scale and found it was easier to move the piece numerous times without the added fear of breaking it. I clean my pieces by lightly washing them with a wet sponge. If the piece is dirty or not dry when the underglaze is applied, the carving pulls both the slip and the underglaze from the piece.

After your piece is clean and dry, apply multiple thin layers of underglaze by either spraying or brushing. I prefer to spray because I'm able to achieve more depth, blending, and fading with the colors, not to mention it allows me to control

Rise Kappa, 14 in. (36 cm) in height, thrown and altered stoneware, with sprayed and brushed underglazes, slip, glaze, and luster, fired to cone 6 in an electric kiln. I typically apply another special effects glaze and refire the piece, to create another layer.

Bisque ware piece sprayed with underglazes and ready for the application of slip.

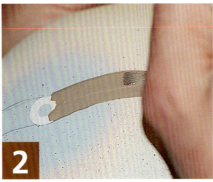

Beginning of the brush application of the slip on the lid of the piece.

While working quickly, begin to carve your design into the wet slip.

Sanding of the finished and dry carved slip. Using delicate pressure.

the amount of underglaze and it distributes evenly. I use a Paashe Type L spray gun connected to a small seven gallon air compressor. Occasionally I'll thin the underglaze with a small amount of water and only strain through a 60 mesh screen if chunks are visible. I've found that setting the pressure at 40 to 60 psi works the best, depending on the area to be covered and the amount of detail needed. More specifically, I use 40 psi for detail and 60 psi for larger areas. It's important that the underglaze is applied thin by working slowly building up the layers. I work with Amaco Velvet underglazes and have found that they are extremely durable and very versatile.

I always start spraying my pieces using the color or colors I want to show through under the slip, then I work up additional layers, from light to dark (figure 1). You'll discover that this becomes a process in itself. Through many attempts you'll see the colors that work best, as well as the new colors that are created by applying them on top of each other. There isn't really a limit of how many layers of underglazes you can use, as it's your personal preference; however, it's possible that having very thick underglaze layers can cause the slip coating to crack. It should be noted, that using just one color can work just as well as multiple colors.

Once I've applied all the colors, I let the piece dry overnight. The process will work sooner, if you prefer, but it's important to make sure all underglazes are dry and not cool to the touch. Once the underglazes are dry, it's time to incorporate the engobes.

Adding Engobes

Commercial engobes traditionally work very well, but I prefer a recipe from Daniel Rhodes (see page 14). I thin the slip to where it will drip once or twice off a dipped brush, then apply it to a small area. When the slip layer is thin, it's easier to build up your layers, you have more time to work, and it's easier to carve into the surface. If you don't use enough slip, the carving area appears washed out, while too much slip can cause the carved slip to crack and pop off. Adding stains to the slip for coloring can also yield some interesting effects and a nice contrast. Some stains don't work as well in the process.

Working in a small area, build up 2 to 3 thin layers of slip. As you can see, I sometimes use a simple round sticker that acts as a guide and template (figure 2).

After the slip is applied onto bisqueware, it'll dry very fast (approximately one to two minutes), but once it dries you can't carve into it to reveal the underglazes, so you need to work in small sections and make your carving marks quickly. If necessary, lightly wetting the slip again with a small brush load of water gives you an extra minute or two; however, I suggest avoiding this, be-

5

Dust off the finish, sanded, carved design. A simple, dry paint brush will work quite nicely.

6

The piece, now finished with the carving, sanding, and cleaning, is ready to be glazed.

7

Spraying the finished piece from multiple angles to completely coat the surface with clear glaze.

8

After firing to cone 6, the different underglazes and the slip/underglaze sgraffito pattern are clearly visible.

81

Recipes

Daniel Rhodes Engobe
Cone 6

Borax	5 %
Custer Feldspar	25
Ball Clay	25
EPK Kaolin	25
Silica	20
Total	**100 %**

Add: Zircopax . . . . 5 %

Apply a thin coat to bisque ware. Thicker applications are prone to cracking or flaking off. Colorants may be added to this base white recipe if desired.

Chun Clear
Cone 6

Whiting	14 %
Zinc Oxide	12
Soda Feldspar	38
OM4 Ball Clay	6
Silica	30
Total	**100 %**

From Leah Leitson, *Ceramics Monthly*, June 2003

---

cause it can affect the final look of the design.

I carve my designs with a two-sided knitting tool, which allows for carving an assortment of dimensions. A variety of instruments like a needle tool, pen or pencil will work as well. The level of intensity of the underglaze color is controlled by the pressure you use to carve; when pressing lightly you only reach the top layer, and by pressing hard you have the ability to reach the bottom or first layer (figure 3). This takes some practice, but with patience you'll find what works best for you and gives you the most interesting results.

Once your design is complete, let the slip dry. Again this happens fast, so you can usually start the next step fairly quickly. Wearing a respirator, sand the raised areas of the carved slip, using steel wool (figure 4). Care should also be taken to avoid sanding anything other than the slip design. The underglaze is tough, but if sanded too hard, it can be removed or scratched.

It's important to note that if you don't sand, you won't have a smooth surface; the areas you carved will rise and have jagged edges. It's also imperative to make sure you remove all sanding dust once you're finished. A simple way to do this is with a standard small dry paint brush (figure 5). The finished, sanded, and dust-free piece is ready to glaze (figure 6).

Glazing

The final step is to coat the piece with a clear glaze. The goal here is to make sure you hit every possible angle of the carved slip. I personally choose to spray the entire piece (figure 7); however, there are a variety of techniques that can be used, including brushing, spraying, dipping or sponging. If brushing is your preferred method of application, I recommend sponging a light first layer, and once dry, continuing with multiple layers of brushing so you avoid disturbing the layers of underglaze. My preference is to spray on the clear glaze as thick as possible on the slip carved portions, as this application sets the slip and assists in the adhering process. If you decide to spray your glaze, be sure to wear a respirator and work in a well-ventilated area throughout the process.

I choose to fire to cone 6, but this process works at all temperatures. This piece was first fired to cone 6 (figure 8) and then more glaze was sprayed on top before it was fired again (see page 12). Be careful as some underglaze and stain colors will burn out at cone 10. It is important to also note that I work with a white clay body, and a darker iron bearing clay body will yield more subtle results.

This process requires immense patience and time, and the ability to accept that not all mistakes are bad. It's well worth the final result if you give it a chance and stick with it.

Block Printing Stamps

by Ann Ruel

Materials List

Block Printing Material
Carving Tool
Interchangeable Gauges
Rolling Pin
Needle Tool
Wide Paint Brush
Smaller Paint Brush
Wire Loop Carving Tool
Putty Knife or Palette Knife
X-Acto Knife or Matt Cutter
Stamp Design

My favorite pottery surface designs involve textures created by carving directly into a piece after it's been formed. I've been experimenting with carving my designs onto block printing material, a flexible eraser-like material that won't crumble, crack or break. In this way, I can test and polish my design choice before I apply it to the clay, and at the same time create a reusable design tool.

Block printing materials are readily available in arts and craft stores or online. There are several sizes and depths of blocks available from which to choose depending on your design (figure 1). In addition, you also need to purchase a carving tool and a few interchangeable gouges. These are usually found alongside the printing blocks.

Purchase three gouges of varying shapes since one will not be sufficient. Get one gouge with a tight V shape to remove a narrow section of debris, a wide U-shaped gouge for removing a wide sweeping amount of debris, and a third gouge with a shape that's in between the other two. As you begin to understand how each of these work, you'll develop preferences for gouges that fit your specific needs.

Decisions, Decisions

The first step to carving the stamp is to decide on your specific design. For the first few stamps, choose bold, blocky designs, as these require only simple carving strokes. As you begin to understand how different variations of gouges affect the overall design, you can become more creative.

There are several ways to work the design onto the surface of the block. You can draw the design directly onto the face of the material using a pencil or use designs from an ink-jet printer, laser printer or newspaper. Images from a printer may need to be traced in pencil before being transferred. Pencil marks can be erased if needed but can also smudge. I prefer creating my design in pencil on a sheet of paper first, and then transferring it to the block.

Line up your design face down on top of the block surface. Rub the back of the paper with a blunt edged object until the carbon transfers completely to the surface. Instructions on the block state that you can run a warm iron over the top of the design to transfer the image.

Before beginning to carve the block, pay special attention to the stamp's edges. Decide whether a border is more appropriate to your

Ceramic Arts Handbook

1 Block printing materials come in a variety of different thicknesses.

2 Use the U-shaped gouge to carve the center braid design. The tight V-shaped nib creates the border lines.

3 Stamp more images than you actually need so you will be able to choose the images with the best quality.

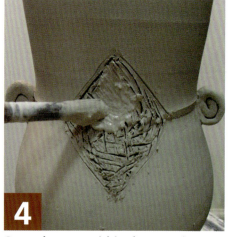

4 Score the area within the traced outline on your pot then use a wide paint brush to apply slip.

purposes or if your design will continue off the edges to become a part of a more complicated pattern.

Carving the Block

Low-relief and high-relief carvings can be created using block printing material. Low-relief carving includes simply gouging ditches along outlines or shallow gouging away from the positive design areas (figure 2). These techniques result in one, level positive shape protruding slightly from the clay surface. High-relief carving involves a more complicated approach where areas of the stamped design sharply protrude from the base of the clay at many different levels. To achieve this look, make some cuts in to the block deeper than others, based on your design.

Surface
Glaze & Form

5 Adhere the stamped slab to the pot. Make sure that all areas, especially the edges and corners, are tightly bonded.

6 This design intentionally runs off the edges of the stamp so that it can be used to create a repeating pattern.

7 Stamped slabs were used to create the body of this Victorian style box.

Remember that the farther you cut into the surface of the block, the more the resulting clay will jut out once stamped.

After carving the design of the stamp, use a sharp edged blade to cut a straight line or beveled edge along the stamp edges to create a border. Before using the stamp on a prepared piece, be sure to test it out on scrap clay first (figure 3). It's easy to become confused and accidentally gouge away the positive space of your design when you should have removed the negative areas or vice-a-versa. Unfortunately if this is the case, the stamped image will result in the reverse of what you intended and you may need to start over. On the other hand, you may notice that an area needs just a little more definition.

Stamping Strategies

You'll find that many different looks can be achieved from one stamp. By varying the contact pressure to the stamp when applying it on the clay surface, you can control design texture. The least amount of pressure results in less definition from your carving and you get a smoother surface. When you apply more pressure, the opposite is true and more texture results. If you want to ensure consistent pressure to the entire stamp at one time, attach the stamp to an

85

acrylic or wooden block for easier use. You can also achieve a varied look after the clay has been stamped by altering the border lines around the stamp.

Indirect Application

There are two techniques for applying the block printing stamp to pottery—indirect application and direct application. When indirectly applying the stamp, keep in mind that not all pottery is conducive to this technique. Objects that tend to flare out as they get taller, such as bowls, do not do as well. Stamps applied to the exterior of the bowls, generally fire without any problems, but sometimes the stamped area tries to flatten out when fired, thus causing the bowl to warp. Cylindrical shapes have less trouble.

To indirectly apply the stamp, roll out a slab of clay between ½-inch and ¾-inch thickness and smooth with a rib. The slab must not be too wet or it may stick to the stamp and you won't get a good impression. Stamp more images than you need and decide which ones to use. Let the clay firm up just enough so it won't distort when removing it from the worktable.

Take a wide putty knife and cut around the edges of the stamped pattern and remove the extra clay. Slowly and carefully, run the putty knife under the clay to release it from the work surface, again being careful not to distort the edges of your pattern.

Using a small looped carving tool, carefully create grooves in the back of the pattered slab, similar to the back of commercial tiles. This makes it lighter and also serves to score the back of the clay.

Place the stamped slab over the area on your pottery where you want to apply it. With a needle tool, trace a light line around the outside border. Remove the slab and generously slip the back of the stamped image. Then, working within the tracing that you made on your pottery, score and slip that area as well (figure 4). Press the image to the clay, beginning gently at the center of the stamp and working out towards the edges. Be sure that your edges are tightly adhered to the surface of the piece or it may peel away during firing (figure 5). Remove any excess slip from the edges with a small paint brush and carefully smooth the area.

Direct Application

Directly applying the stamp to a piece is much more complicated as you risk distorting your piece or weakening a wall. Try applying the stamps to clay slabs that have been placed in a mold or directly apply the stamp to a slab and use this to create pattern pieces to be assembled. Block printing stamps can be cut so that when used in multiples they can form creative patterns (figure 6). I created four of these textured slabs (figure 7), cut them into squared pattern pieces and assembled them into a Victorian box with a lid.

Grouting for Effect

by Laura Reutter

Reverie, after grouting. 17 in. (43 cm) in height, press-molded stoneware, glaze, black grout, fired to cone 6.

Adding grout to tiles, mosaics, and tile installations can enhance a design, strengthen linear elements, and even create a stained-glass effect. Furthermore, grout can impart a patina to glazed tiles, producing an aged or weathered appearance. Grouting for effect isn't a new idea—several tile companies around the turn of the last century used grout in decorative as well as functional ways, including Moravian Tile Works and the Hartford Faience Company.

Grout

Grout is a mixture of cement, sand, and colorant to which water is added. Like mortar, grout hardens slowly over a period of time. In conventional tile installations, grout fills the spaces between ceramic pieces, creating a smooth durable surface that prevents the penetration of moisture and dirt. Grout is available in a wide range of premixed colors, making it easy for artists to pick and choose the appropriate hue for their project.

To achieve a decorative effect, tiles require recessed areas in their surface that will hold grout. These recessed areas may be linear elements such as grooves or negative shapes carved into the tile. Grout is applied to the tile after the glaze firing. Gaps between whole tiles and tile mosaics also create grout lines. Depending on the width of the grout line, the effect can range from subtle to dramatic.

The following examples focus on using charcoal black grout applied to the surface of glazed stoneware tiles that have been fired to cone 6.

Narrow Lines

The swan tile is a simple 4×8-inch tile based on an Art Nouveau period design. First roll out a ½-inch thick

Ceramic Arts Handbook

1 Remove excess glaze with a pointed tool from all areas that will receive grout.

2 Necessary tools: plastic drop cloth, gloves, containers, water, sponge, stir stick, grout, and squeegee.

3 Apply grout to the tile surface with a flexible tool. Wear protective gloves.

4 Carefully sponge off excess grout after it has set up.

5 Swan tile after grouting, showing altered glaze colors.

6 Carve grout lines deep enough to provide plenty of 'grab'.

slab of clay that's large enough to accommodate the design. Make the paper pattern slightly larger than the final tile size to allow for shrinkage during drying and firing. Transfer the image to the clay slab by tracing over the paper pattern with a pencil, pressing firmly to ensure the design is inscribed into the clay.

Cut the slab to its desired size and allow it to stiffen overnight. Once the clay is almost leather hard, incise narrow lines—approximately 1/16-inch wide and 1/8-inch deep—around the primary shapes on the clay tile. Use a combination of wooden and metal clay modeling tools and bamboo skewers to create the lines. Add additional linear details to the swan tile, such as feathers and ripples in the water, if desired. Keep in mind that the wider and deeper the incised line, the more grout it will hold and the more prominent the grout line becomes. Extremely shallow details will not retain the grout.

Brush, pour or dip glazes onto the tile, taking care not to fill the grooves. After glazing but before firing, any glaze drips that have settled into the grooves must be removed using a needle tool or pointed wooden stick (figure 1). Grout won't stick in a shallow groove that's par-

The cone 6 glaze-fired stoneware *Idyll* tile (10x8 in.), before adding grout to the incised lines.

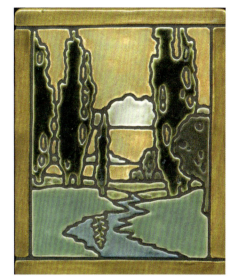

Idyll after grouting. The black grout defines the different elements of the landscape.

tially filled with glaze. Once the tile has been glaze fired, it's ready to accept grout.

Note: Colored grout stains everything it touches! Protect your work area with plastic sheeting or newsprint and wear gloves. In addition to the grout, available in home centers and flooring stores, you'll also need a sponge, container of water, container for grout, stirring stick, and a flexible squeegee for application (figure 2). Mix the grout as instructed by the manufacturer and apply to the surface of the tile.

I like to use a flexible rubber pottery rib to push the grout firmly in all directions over the tile (figure 3). Make sure the grout penetrates into the bottom of every groove. The surface and sides of the tile should be completely covered with grout so that any color changes are consistent overall.

Once the lines are filled, the grout should be left undisturbed in order to set up. After 30 minutes or so, sponge off any excess grout. Use a slightly damp sponge and be careful not to lift grout out of the grooves (figure 4). If you do accidentally remove too much grout, you can add a little where needed at this time.

There will probably be some alteration of glaze colors during grouting. Light glazes and matte glazes are especially prone to picking up colors from grout. Test a sample of your glaze with some grout first if you want to avoid unexpected color shifts. Areas that are sensitive to staining may be coated with a resist such as paste wax or varnish prior to applying grout. Again, testing is recommended.

I found that the white glaze on the swan's body was readily stained by the black grout, but I wanted the grayish muted effect that resulted and did not mask this color (figure 5).

Moderate Lines

My *Idyll* tile was designed specifically to utilize black grout lines that would strengthen the composition, enhancing an already linear Arts and Crafts-style image.

The first step is to establish a basic pattern on paper. Use a wide-tipped permanent marker over a pre-existing drawing to give an idea of how the final grout lines will look. Trace the pattern using a stylus, transferring the design to a stiffened clay slab. Once the design is established on the slab, carve grooves to a width and depth of at least $1/8$ inch (figure 6). The grout requires a groove deep enough to anchor it, ensuring it will stay in place during application and sponging.

As described above, apply grout liberally and use firm pressure in all directions. Sponging off the grout reveals dramatic changes in the appearance of the tile.

The finished tile will probably appear darker and/or more muted than the original due to coloration from the grout. This is normal and part of the charm of the process. The addition of black grout lines strengthens this composition greatly. Compare the photograph of *Idyll* before and after grouting.

Wide Lines

My goal in designing *Reverie* was to produce an effect similar to a stained glass window. Strong grout lines form an integral part of the composition much like lead lines do in stained glass.

Reverie is a multi-part tile assemblage measuring 12×17×½ inch. Its four press-molded sections have grooves approximately ¼-inch wide and ¼-inch deep to accept grout. The 20 border pieces are made separately from stiff clay slabs cut to size. I used a decorative stamp to impress a rose motif at the corners.

In this example, grout fills the grooves in the tiles, gaps between molded sections, details in the face and hair, as well as filling in the letters of Reverie—producing positive letters from a carved negative space.

For a multi-part project, all the glazed pieces must be adhered to a support before grouting. Suitable supports include plywood, mold resistant drywall, cement board, brick, and concrete. Depending on the support chosen, prep work may be involved, such as sanding painted surfaces. There are tile adhesives available for every need. Check your home center and follow the instructions provided with the adhesive. I prefer to use water-based adhesives, which give off less odor and are easier to clean up. Spacing between sections is an important consideration; it should be consistent and pleasing to the eye. Remember that gaps become dark filled in lines and play a big role in the final appearance of your project. Tile adhesive doesn't set up instantly so you have time to adjust the placement of individual pieces if you don't like the initial placement.

Word Decoration

by Connie Norman

Connie Norman uses letterpress patterns as a signature design element.

My current style of working all started one day during a workshop. The man standing next to me smiled and secretly showed me some hole reinforcements labels. (You know, the little white round things that go around paper for three ring binders). He was acting as if he was showing me a secret family recipe. He was using them for glaze decoration and after I saw that, I was in hot pursuit of office supplies. Texture has always been important to me, but I now use it in a subtler form. I balance text as pattern and texture, with passages of color and line. The text in my pieces acts as a path to look inward, a glimpse into my private thoughts, which at times are playful and at others are much darker in tone.

I create architectural vessels using slab construction. All my forms are made with glazing in the forefront of my mind. Although every step of my process is extremely time consuming, the glazing takes the longest.

Making the Form

To begin, make paper templates for each side of the vessel, including the bottom. You can use tag board, although it doesn't hold up very long, or you can use tar paper from your local home store.

Roll out ½-inch thick slabs. I like this thickness because the slabs support themselves when attached. Compress the slabs with a rib, this weaves the clay particles together to give the slab a stronger working strength, and makes them fairly smooth.

After the side slabs are leather hard (the bottom slab should be kept to a slight softer leather hard), use your templates to cut out the pieces of the vessel. Tip: Cut each slab edge with a bevel to help join the corners together. Score and slip heavily, attach two of the beveled sides together, creating a 90° angle, then repeat with the other two sides. After you have two "L" shapes or two halves, place these together and join

Ceramic Arts Handbook

1. Score and slip the beveled edges of each slab heavily and add a reinforcement coil to the seam.

2. To make the bottom of the vessel, flip it upside down, lay the slab on top of the arch, and join.

3. A Surform tool refines the shape of the vessel by removing extra clay from the reinforcement coils.

4. Trim the extra clay off the rim using a fettling knife and clean up the edges.

5. Press letterpress type into the clay to create a pattern with shape and line.

6. Wipe the extra glaze off the text with a sponge, making sure it remains in the recessed patterns.

the remaining beveled edges to create a box. Add a thick reinforcement coil to the joints (figure 1). The reinforcement coil is very important because of all the handling of the slabs from this point on. Finish the edges by blending in the coils and then smooth out the form.

Attaching the Bottom and Lip

Turn the vessel upside down and attach a bottom with a softer leather-hard piece—it should be flexible enough to stretch around the vessel if you have a curved foot or rim (figure 2). Once the reinforcement coils for the bottom are blended in, everything needs to firm up again.

When everything is leather-hard, use a Surform to refine the shape and remove any extra clay from the reinforcement coils (figure 3). Remove the Surform texture with a rubber rib. The smoother you get the clay the better the decorating and glazing will go. Once the clay can support its own weight, flip it over carefully and add a lip or rim to the vessel (figure 4). The original template, used to cut out the sides and the bottom, is used again to create the arch at the top of the pot. Use the pattern piece to draw the curve, then cut off the excess clay. Follow by adding one-inch slabs to the top to create the finished rim.

7 Tape off the dry, glazed text with masking tape. Press and seal the tape well to prevent glaze leaks.

8 Use fine-line auto-body tape to make thin lines on the bisque ware.

9 Punch holes into stickers to add additional decoration to your pieces.

10 Apply stickers onto the bisque to create a pattern or layered design.

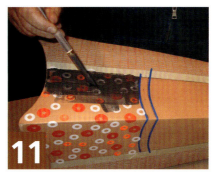
11 Brush three even coats of glaze over the applied stickers and allow the glaze to dry.

12 Use an X-Acto knife to peel off the stickers before you glaze fire.

Glazing

After bisque firing, brush glaze into the text, and wipe off the excess with a sponge (figure 6). Then glaze the inside by pouring glaze in, rolling it around to cover all the sides, then pouring out the excess. Because the vessel is now saturated with water from the sponging and glazing, it needs to dry at least 24 hours before continuing. This is important because if the bisque is damp, the masking tape won't stick to it.

I love how the shiny and the matte surfaces of bare clay play off each other. Mask off the sections that will remain bare, including all the text sections that already have glaze (figure 7). The beauty of masking tape is that you can draw on the bisque because the tape is translucent enough to see the pencil marks. I find the pencil drawings helpful with making registration marks. If you don't like drawing on bisque ware you can draw on the masking tape instead. Leave the tape on the text section during the entire glazing process.

The best tape to use for thin lines of decoration is Scotch Fine Line Tape (figure 8). This tape is polypropylene plastic film, and it adheres well to the bisque, makes a very clean line, and also works well for curved lines. It can be found in automotive stores in the paint section.

When first creating glaze resist shapes I started with plain office supplies—whatever my local store had available. I then started hole punching the round circles and looking for other ways to alter my office supplies (figure 9 and 10).

Once you finish applying tape and other resist shapes, brush on three coats of glaze, making sure to change directions of your brush strokes to ensure even coverage (figure 11). Peel off the tape and adhesive decorations before the glaze firing (figure 12). Make sure to remove the entire sticker and all the tape. If any adhesive from the sticker remains on the bisque, it leaves a residue and does not burn away in the kiln. Glaze fire to your clay body's temperature.

Recipes

Hirsh Satin Base
Cone 04-02

Gerstley Borate	32 %
Lithium Carbonate	9
Whiting	17
Nepheline Syenite	4
EPK Kaolin	4
Silica	34
Total	100 %

Excellent Black
Cone 04

Lithium Carbonate	9 %
Wollastonite	14
Ferro Frit 3195	43
EPK Kaolin	23
Silica	11
Total	100 %
Add: Bentonite	2
Black Iron Oxide	2
Black Mason Stain	2
Cobalt Oxide	2

Black Tar
Cone 04

Borax	39 %
Gerstley Borate	50
Silica	11
Total	100 %
Add: Red Iron Oxide	10
Cobalt Carbonate	15
Iron chromate	15
Black Copper Oxide	10
Rutile	10

Jacquie's Crimson
Cone 04

Gerstley Borate	38.0%
Lithium Carbonate	10.0
Nepheline Syenite	5.0
EPK Kaolin	5.0
Silica	42.0
Total	100.0%
Add: Crimson Stain	10.0
Veegum	1.5

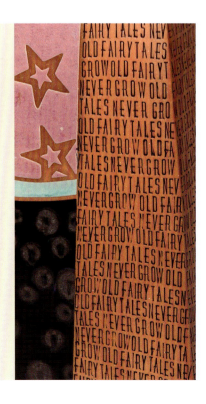

The Lettering

I use old letterpress type to make my texture and patterns. Rubber stamps don't work because they are not hard enough, so if possible, try to avoid them. Use a rubber tipped clay shaper to draw guide lines for the text. The clay shaper will lay down a light line without marring the surface. Decide how to divide up the vessel to then add text. As the surface is divided, think about what enhances the form vertically, horizontally, and three dimensionally.

A Painterly Approach

by Tim Ludwig

Surface Glaze&Form

Tim Ludwig's work combines expressive forms and a layered surface of textures and images inspired by historical botanical illustrations. Photo: Randall Smith.

About 10 years ago, I started to feel that it was time to change my work, and that I wanted more control over the surface. This came after nearly 30 years of making work, and for a time finishing it in salt, wood, primitive, and saggar firings. So, I enrolled in a summer class at Arrowmont School of Crafts in Gatlinburg, Tennessee. The instructor, Bede Clarke, was using slips with stains to create a surface that was astonishing. My life, and my work was about to change. Using what I learned about creating these surfaces, I started integrating them with the loose vessel forms I had developed over many years, forms influenced by the 1960's abstract expressionist, Pete Voulkos, and everyone else who thought it was okay to make crooked pots.

Choosing the images for the surface became the focus for about a year. I moved from animals, to figurative subjects, and then to plants. I settled on botanical illustrations from the 1700-1800's, from my admiration of those artists who set forth throughout the world seeking flowers to paint and illustrate and to sneak in a little artistic license.

The beauty of this process is that I did not have to change the way I was making pots. I decided on an earthenware body that I have used for fifteen plus years. The slip recipe was from Bede and has proved to be very compatible with my clay, stains, and firing. If you decide on a different firing temperature or clay color, there are clay and slip formulas that work just as well; use what you're comfortable with, or have already tested. If you're starting from the beginning and looking for compatible recipes or commercial products, remember to test, test, and test some more before you leap in and start working on finished pieces.

I learned very quickly to take good notes, measure, weigh, and test when it comes to creating the colored slips I use.. The painting process can take many hours of hard work, so don't leave it to guessing.

1 Add cheesecloth dipped in the slip to create an additional visual and tactile layer.

2 Begin drawing the image with a needle tool and/or a sharp pencil. Draw in details last.

3 Work with one color family at a time. A base green is mixed with other stains creating a value scale.

4 Painting the leaves, laying down a layer of a light green first.

5 Create the shading using a colored slip mixture of a slightly darker value.

6 Work through the value scale using combinations of your slip choices to develop depth.

I mix 1000 gram batches of the base slip (see recipe on page 25) to a consistency of mayonnaise, which provides a good starting thickness to cover the surface of the piece and to begin mixing with the stains to produce a color palette. Test your colors before committing to using them on a piece.

Priming the Surface
Generally I throw four to five pieces at a time. When the pieces are a little shy of leather hard, I brush two coats of the base slip across the surface, leaving the red clay slightly exposed in small areas for aesthetic purposes. Then, when the slip has dried, these pieces are covered with plastic and put away in a storage cabinet or damp box to be worked on individually at an appropriate time.

On the surface of some of the pieces, I add cheesecloth dipped in the slip to create an additional visual and tactile layer. The cheesecloth burns out in the bisque and leaves behind a raised impression (figure 1).

Painting the Image
Before I start mapping out the image, I add colored slip to the certain areas (see the yellow areas of the background in figure 2). Once the slip has lost its sheen, I draw the image into the soft, leather-hard surface with

7 Clean out the incised lines occasionally during the painting process using a fettling knife.

8 Create a value scale for the flower colors on a clean piece of Plexiglas.

9 Paint the flower petals using a smaller brush, again working on one section at a time.

10 Create shadows and highlights following the same method used to create the leaves.

a needle tool and/or a sharp pencil (figure 2).

When I'm ready to start painting, I measure out the base color, in this case green, on a piece of clean Plexiglas and create a value scale by mixing in additional stains using a palette knife (figure 3). I begin painting the image, usually the leaves first, and refine any of the drawing at this time. I use the drawn lines as a guide as I paint (figure 4). The lines define the edges and veins of the leaves and petals, and mark where the shading and highlights of the image shift or change. Blending of the slip can be achieved with a good brush; I use Kolinsky sable, and have found that a smooth transition across the given value scale is accomplished with patience (figure 5). Start with a light to medium shade, and then add highlights and shadows. Here you can see one of the completed leaves with the shadows and dimension added using the different shades (figure 6).

As I paint, I will stop occasionally and clean out the incised lines with a thin fettling knife (figure 7). I've found that the needle tool does not work well as it leaves small clay grubbies or crumbs on the surface.

Similar to how a plant grows, after I finish with the leaves and any

Recipes

Red Earthenware Body

Newman's Red Clay	35 %
Redart Clay	35
Ball Clay	10
Fireclay	10
Talc	10
	100 %

Add: Medium Grog......10 %

This body suits my needs for throwing and firing, you may want to use a smoother clay, or try this recipe with finer grog or no grog to suit your purposes.

Stephenson's Slip

EPK Kaolin	12.5 %
Tile 6	12.5
Ball Clay	25.0
Ferro Frit 3124	20.0
Talc	5.0
Silica	20.0
Pyrotol	5.0
	100.0 %

Add: Zircopax........10.0 %

This slip has been very stable with the clay body I use and is quite compatible with the stains. You may want to add glycerol to the slip/stain mix on the palette to improve the viscosity for brushing.

other darker tones, I continue on to the flower of the plant, measuring out the base color onto the Plexiglas palette and creating a value scale again (figure 8), then painting the image in the same way (figure 9). Unlike painting with glazes, the finished, unfired slip image will be close to the colors of the final, fired piece, especially if you use commercial stains as colorants (figure 10). These stains have been fired as part of the manufacturing process, and so the color you see is close to the final color that will be produced, depending on the surface you paint onto, the firing temperature, and whether or not you choose to glaze the piece. Check with the manufacturer to see what temperature individual stains can be fired to before the color starts to burn out.

After I've finished creating and cleaning up the image, the platter is fired to cone 04 for the bisque. After firing, I mix a clear, satin, commercial glaze in a 50/50 ratio with water and spray a very thin coat onto the bisque ware. The piece is refired to cone 06. This final firing allows the color to brighten and intensify in comparison to the bisque stage.

Tips for Branching Out

Take time to refine your technique and find subject matter that engages you. Using slips to paint images on clay has been around a long time; if the process interests you, look around to find examples to be inspired by.

Matching the image with the form is extremely important. You can't compensate for a bad form via surface decoration or firing. The image and form should respond to one another; do not just make an object to paint. I have become much more comfortable with my decision to create the work shown here. It's hard and takes a lot of time to complete a piece, so be prepared if you plan to adopt a similar method.

I mix up small quantities of the colored slips in 300 gram batches, using 5–20% stain depending on the color. I store them in small resealable containers and take them out as I need to paint each piece. I keep my dry stains in a nuts and bolts cabinet. The drawers make them easy to access, and the clear plastic allows me to see the colors.

Mix small quantities of stained slips. Here 300 gram batches are prepared with 5–20% stain, based on tests of each color.

Storing dry stains in a cabinet with clear drawers allows for easy access, good visibility and organization by color family.

Using the Correct Brush

by Michael Harbridge

Clay artists can spend a great deal of time creating unique shapes only to suffer disappointment with the final project because the glaze finish comes out streaky or blotchy. Selecting the proper brush is an important part of the creative process and knowing what to look for in a brush can alleviate frustration.

With literally thousands of different brushes on the market in a variety of sizes, styles, and hair types, where do you begin to narrow the search? While the pack of large brushes from the dollar store may be appealing from the price standpoint, it may not be the best option. The kind of hair, shape, and length of the bristle will have a dramatic effect on the final outcome.

Brush Hair

In most cases, soft bristles are the preference when applying engobes, ceramic colorants and glazes. If a bristle is too stiff, it will drag, spreading colors or glazes too thin.

You'll generally find three different kinds of bristle options. Synthetic hair is a manufactured product often made of nylon and can have a plastic feel. The thickness of the bristle will make a big difference in how well the brush performs. Many inexpensive brushes have thick, stiff plastic bristles. These brushes will not hold or apply color well. The rough, jagged ends of the hairs will likely leave streaks in the colors. Quality synthetics have finer hair, are much softer and the bristles come to a nice point.

Natural hair brushes are usually the best option for glazing. However, not all types of natural hair brushes will work. While hog bristle brushes are made with natural hairs, these stiff, white hairs are not the best option for glazing. Goat hair is also a white bristle but has a plush, soft feel and is a favorite for many artists. Badger hair and blends of soft hair like squirrel also make fine brushes for use with engobes and glazes.

The final type is a blend of natural and synthetic bristles. These brushes vary, depending upon the combination of hairs. Some natural bristles are soft and limp when loaded with glaze. By adding some firmer synthetic or natural bristles within the soft hairs, the brush can hold its shape better and give nice coverage.

Shape and Size

You may not think the shape of a brush would make a difference. Pick up a fan brush and a flat brush with the same hair and run your fingers across the bristles. The bristles in the flat brush are probably packed tighter and have a shorter length. Even though the hair is the same, the fan will lay the color on better. Will a #2 flat perform differently than a #12 flat? Absolutely! The numbers on brushes refer to the size, with

Surface Glaze&Form

Left: Stiff fan brush
One coat of glaze applied with this stiff, natural hog hair bristle, fan shaped brush left a streaky finish.

Right: Badger hair fan brush
Badger hair holds lots of color and does a great job of depositing smooth layers of color. One coat of glaze applied using this brush gave good coverage and had less texture.

Left: Small flat synthetic brush. While these synthetic brushes have soft bristles, the small size and tightly bound hairs don't hold as much color as a fan and require more frequent loading. One coat of glaze came out streaky.

Right: Large flat synthetic brush. The larger size of this brush helped give a little better coverage than the smaller version on the right.

Left: Soft goat hair hake brush. Hake brushes are ideal for glazing and come in a variety of sizes. The soft hair holds a lot of glaze and layers nicely.

Right: Dollar store synthetic brush. This inexpensive brush has thick plastic bristles. It was difficult to get this brush to cover the surface with glaze because the coarse hairs scraped and dragged the color, leaving a very streaky finish.

numbers increasing as the brush size increases. Many artists use a larger brush on the main area and a smaller version of the same brush to go around details. It's possible they'll get streaks or starved glaze areas where the smaller brush is used because the brush doesn't hold as much color and it requires more frequent loading. The artist is also making many more short strokes rather than long, gliding motions.

It's always best to use the largest brush possible. If a smaller brush is required for fine work areas, watch to be sure the brush is being loaded well and the colors or glazes are being applied evenly. Brushes like the hake and soft fans are ideal for covering large areas. They usually lay the color or glaze on well without dragging through and creating streaks.

Stiffer fans are perfect for textured or thick engobes, colorants, and glazes because they require a brush capable of lifting and holding the products. Soft goat hair fans are too limp and will have a difficult time picking up thick or textured glazes and spreading them evenly. Stiffer brushes also reach down into highly textured or detailed spots. It may work best to apply the first coat on textured items with a stiff fan and apply subsequent coats with a softer brush. Using a stiff brush for all coats could result in the colors filling in the crevices, while actually dragging and pulling the color from the high points or tips of the texture, leaving a starved area.

Chinese Brush Painting

by Elizabeth Priddy

This piece, **Egret Moon**, is one in a series of tile paintings made using Chinese brush painting techniques.

Chinese brush painting uses specific brushes, brush strokes, and color loading methods. My painting has the character and color depth of traditional china painting but uses techniques of rice paper brush painting. I use true-color, blending underglazes on white stoneware clay and only one glaze firing is required. The painting itself is layered between a satin white base glaze and a glossy clear glaze, both of which must fit well with the clay body. After firing, the image looks as though it's trapped in glass. The painting stains the translucent glossy glaze, making an integrated surface that has more visual depth than paintings done over a matt slip.

Painting directly onto a base glaze also allows for easy erasing with a palette knife or a bamboo skewer. Since glaze particles are fine enough to lift away cleanly, the top layer of a tinted glaze or an individual section can be pulled away, revealing fine lines of white glaze. In contrast, engobes or slips leave ragged edges when the top painting is removed.

Commercial underglazes work like tubes of liquid watercolors. Paint with the underglazes straight from the jar. As you clean your brush between strokes, enough water remains for loading and blending the color. I use just seven colors to create the entire palette in my pieces: black, white, yellow, red, blue, dark green, and brown.

This technique can be adapted for oxidation or reduction firing and for temperature ranges from earthenware to stoneware. If you want to maintain optimal clarity of color, then choose a white clay, zinc-free glazes, and fire the pieces in an electric kiln.

Strokes and Loads

I mainly use five strokes, four loads, and dian or shaped dots made with the brush tip. The five strokes are bone, grass, vertical, side, and calligraphy. The loads are base, five-color, moon, and bamboo. Base load is one color throughout the brush, five-color is a base of water, then each color loaded in sequence and proportionally, starting with the lightest color at the base of the brush and ending with the darkest color in the tip. The brush is flattened at the tip for the moon load and after loading the brush with one color, one edge of the tip is dipped in black. Bamboo load is the same as the moon load, only the black is dipped along both edges of a flattened brush and blended to make a shaded stroke resulting in a rounded tube mark; this is the load for the bone stroke, which looks like a short bone with rounded ends.

A hake brush is used for applying fields and washes of color. Two colors are loaded onto the brush and blended by brushing back and forth on a flat surface to create a fade.

For dimensional dots, select a brush that is large enough to cover half the width of the dot. Place the brush light side to the center and swirl the brush around to meet itself.

Edges of forms, banding, or dropped shadows are made with a moon loaded, or half-bamboo stroke. It is made on a compound brush that is flattened before loading.

The bone stroke is used to show rounded or hollow forms. The load is dark on both sides of a flattened brush. Jiggle the brush to widen and finish the stroke at each end.

Grass strokes are for calligraphy and detailed line drawing. Even in simple drawing, variation in pressure of the point is used to create thick and thin lines within one stroke.

The marks across the top show how each color is added and blended into the brush for a five color load. The bottom stroke which is called a vertical stroke shows varied color and lines as the brush drags through.

Brushes

The main component of brush painting is the special technique of mixing and blending color directly in an absorbent, natural hair, compound brush. Chinese bamboo mounted brushes come to perfect points that can be reshaped to create special effects or strokes. I use a variety of sizes and hair compositions. The round bamboo handle allows the brush to twirl and dance or be gripped tightly for miniscule detail work. The hair bundle is arranged in the ferrule with the very absorbent core hair and stiff hairs for spring at the center. Softer, smoother, oilier hair surrounds the core to retain moisture and direct the paint to the point. Hair varies by quality of absorption and color from goat to weasel, deer, fox, or horse. Flat goat hair hake brushes are used for washes and applying glaze. Many brushes marketed to potters are only good for base loaded grass and calligraphy marks. They do not have the springy quality that is necessary for bone and vertical stroke. Expect to pay about $25 for the essential Chinese painting tool, the compound brush.

Practice Makes Perfect

To begin, practice on rice paper with ink to get to know your brushes, loads, and strokes. Also, test on examples of your materials and try the stroke techniques before completing entire pieces.

When you're ready to start painting on clay, try starting with an image like the one of the egret and moon demonstrated here. Glaze a slab tile with the satin white glaze. Allow a space for the moon in the clay frame. Cover the moon area with a paper resist and wash in the sky and ground using a hake brush (figure 1).

Paint the moon in using the moon load with white, yellow, and black. The clean side of the tip is presented to the interior of the moon shape and the black side is swept in a circle around the exterior to meet itself. This is a vertical stroke using a large brush equal to the size of the radius of the circle. This creates a dimensional dot. It's used for any fleshy shapes with fullness like eyes, grapes, cherries, moons, or rounded shells (figure 2).

Create the neck of the egret using a bamboo load with gray at the center and black edges. By applying pressure down and then lifting up part way, the head is formed and extended into the neck of the bird with one fluid vertical stroke. This defines the plumbing pipe shape of the neck that distinguishes an egret from a goose or a swan (figure 3). Each bird has a distinctive quality, usually it's the shape of the beak or plumage, but for egrets, it's their neck at rest.

The body is a side stroke with a moon load. The clean side of the

Ceramic Arts Handbook

1
Paint a wash with a solid loaded hake brush over rice paper masks for the moon and egret shapes.

2
The brush is swept in a circle with the light yellow side to the center of the moon, creating a fade to the outside.

3
A bamboo loaded brush with white at the center and black edges, follows the form of the egret's head and neck.

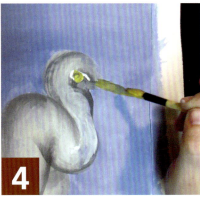

4
A load of white fading to black in the tip rounds out the form of the belly of the bird with a side stroke.

5
A round vertical stroke with a moon load makes the eye. A five color load with a vertical stroke makes the beak.

6
Grass strokes make body feathers. Spread the brush into finger shapes to make multiple marks.

tip faces the interior of the body (see figure 4).

The beak and eye are placed carefully using a three-color load of white, yellow, and black on a small brush and vertical strokes (figure 5).

Feathers are formed with the grass stroke. Dry the clean brush hair on a cloth and twist it to a gnarled head. Drag the splayed hairs through a wet, diluted, gray for a base load of just the tips of the brush. Place, then lift the brush in the same soft motion (figure 6). Define the legs last; scrape through the blue was to reveal the white glaze, then use linked bone strokes and a bamboo load. They must be placed carefully to balance the weight of the completed bird (figure 7).

Lastly, use calligraphy strokes to refine the image and apply detail work in the form of dian or lively shaped dots made with the brush tip. Correct imperfect marks and add lines to the feathers, rocks, and

Surface
Glaze & Form

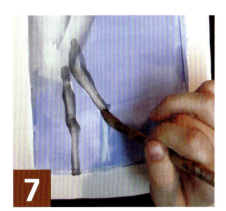

7 Scrape the blue back to reveal white for the legs. Use a small bone stroke and a bamboo load to position legs.

8 A combination of calligraphy strokes, dian and white scratch work refine the image.

9 Scratch in with a bamboo skewer to make white line work details for rocks, grass, and a snail.

10 Coat the painting with clear glaze. Move quickly and lightly.

11 Paint an oil spot black glaze over the black outline to create a dark frame.

the grass (figure 8). Then go back and do white scratch work to place highlights and apply white dian (figure 9).

Apply the top, sealing, clear glossy glaze with a hake brush in one clean swift stroke. Do not rub or hesitate as this will catch and lift the painting off instead of coating it (figure 10). Tip: You can also use a roller to apply the clear glaze.

Use an oil spot black glaze to create the frame around the image and then it is ready to fire to cone 7–8 in an electric kiln (figure 11).

Raku, gas, electric, and wood all require distinct adjustments, but I have found a way with every material set that I have tried. Each surprises me with its own unique quality and beauty.

Painting Styles

There are four basic styles of Chinese brush painting. Baimiao or line work, is most similar to Japanese sumi-e painting. Gongbi, or meticu-

The finished piece, one in a series of paintings with this theme on tiles created with a moon pop-out in the frame.

lous style, is the most common and familiar and is basic flower and bird painting. Mogu, or boneless style, uses no understructure of line work to compose. All shapes and forms come from the load and tone of the brush marks. There are at least 24 shapes of leaves and rocks required for mastery of this technique. While it is evaluated by the full use of the catalog of marks, it is the most free and loose style of painting. As it relies on fades and tonal variation to create form structure, this creates a problem in clay. The color generally stays true but its final intensity can vary according to glaze application or placement in the kiln. Because of this, I paint mainly in the boneless style and then add calligraphy, or line work. These "insurance strokes" guarantee that my compositions hold their structure even if some delicate marks recede during firing. As you practice, you become accomplished at every style, load, and stroke. The ultimate goal of practice with the brush is to pick and choose among those elements freely. When you can do this, it is called Xieyi or scholar's style.

Majolica Decoration

by Jake Allee

I've recently been experimenting with translating my drawings onto ceramic objects using the majolica technique. The direct nature of applying color through this brush technique has a nice appeal because the fired result looks pretty close to the way it was applied. In an effort to get some of my advanced students to expand their experience with different firing ranges, I've been introducing majolica as a way to explore what the character and the color palette this technique has to offer.

For the type of imagery I'm trying to achieve, I've found that simple, refined forms with smooth surfaces are best, but thinking outside of the box might lead you beyond the conventional interpretation of this technique. Consider the variety of textures you can create, combined with alternatives to applying stains using non-traditional techniques. Spattering with a toothbrush, spraying with a squirt bottle, or dabbing with a crumpled rag might be just the beginning.

Majolica's Evolution

Colorful majolica style glazing was most likely the result of Mesopotamian potters' efforts to imitate the surface decoration of Chinese Tang dynasty wares traded into the region. The white tin-glaze style with heavy metal oxides painted on for decoration is seen in Mesopotamia as early as the 9th century. As time went on, the refinement of brush decoration improved and the technique traveled with Moorish culture into Italy, Spain, and Morocco. Since making true, white porcelain historically eluded people outside of China, many cultures used majolica style glazing to achieve intricate and colorful decoration on a bright white background. The influence of Middle-Eastern majolica tech-

When starting to work with majolica glaze techniques, Jake Allee looked to historical pieces from Iznik, as well as Spain and Italy, and adopted a limited color palette of analogous and complementary combinations.

1 Using the banding wheel, bands of stain are applied on the plate to define the edge of the composition.

2 A light wash is applied to the background with a larger brush establishing the upper area of the composition.

3 The same color is established in the mid-ground and foreground working toward a sense of unity through color choice. At this point a horizon line becomes evident.

nique eventually spread all over the world and can be seen as far away as Mexico in colonial wares and even in more contemporary folk ceramics. The finest majolica brush work I have ever seen is on Delft-style tiles commissioned from Holland in the 1600's and installed in churches on the coast of Brazil. Majolica-style glaze is a testament to the power of ceramics as a vehicle for cultural as well as aesthetic interchange.

Applying the Base Glaze

The majolica technique begins with applying an opaque white glaze over your bisque fired clay. I mix my own clay, but also use APS Red from New Mexico Clay. Any cone 04 red clay that works with your glaze base is suitable.

Linda Arbuckle's Majolica Glaze Base works great, but pay attention to the thickness of the glaze when applying it. If it's too thick, it tends to crawl, and if applied too thin it will cause the surface to be dry. For best results, use tongs to dip the pieces and avoid getting finger marks on them, which become very evident when applying the stains. Any drips can be smoothed out with your finger tip after the glaze completely dries on the bisque piece. Use a dust mask when smoothing the dry glaze.

If you don't want to mix your own glaze, many commercial low-fire white glazes will work just as well including Amaco's LG-11 white low-fire glaze and Laguna's EM-2118 Majolica Glaze. Many other stiff white glazes may also work, just do some tests prior to getting started.

Preparing Stains

To prepare the colors, I mix Gerstley borate with commercial stains from Standard Ceramics Supply, including but not limited to K-44 Royal Purple glaze stain, and #496 Christmas Red glaze stain. The Gerstley borate helps the stains to flux and adding 20% of it works great for most stains, although I add 50% to black stain and 40% to chrome green. I

4 Starting back at the top, apply a contrasting color to develop detail using a fine brush.

5 Address the details of the mid- and foreground with the addition of black to create areas of emphasis.

6 A design relating to the rest of the composition is repeated using black in the banded areas.

measure ingredients by volume using a plastic tablespoon and always run a couple of test tiles through a glaze firing before committing to mixing large amounts.

Commercially available stain mixes, such as Amaco's Gloss Decorating Color series (GDC) and Duncan's Concepts Underglazes are listed as suitable for use with majolica. Linda Arbuckle mentions that some Amaco Velvet Underglazes also work, and many other underglazes may as well. Note: Be sure to test any product you plan to use with your clay and glaze, and under your firing conditions before committing to it fully.

Brushes

For this technique, I've been using several sizes of bamboo brushes and small watercolor brushes. One that's long and thin, called an "ex liner" (or "rigger" brush as it's used by watercolor artists to paint the detailed rigging on sailboat images) and another called a "script liner" also used for fine lines and details.

You may wish to consider different marks made by brushes such as the flats and fans. Pay attention to possibilities in the types of mark each type of brush can make, and develop your skill with brushes using India ink on paper before committing to the ceramic material.

Applying Stain

I've been playing with decorating plates lately because they have a nice flat surface that can be treated like a canvas or piece of paper. My watercolor training in school has proved quite effective in approaching composition as well as color. A landscape-style composition is a great place to start.

My first attempts at multi-colored brush decoration turned out pretty disastrous. After looking at what I liked in many different historical styles, I discovered I was using too many colors. Much of the historical work that appealed to me had a stripped down color scheme and relied on white background to cre-

Recipes

Linda Arbuckle's Majolica Glaze Base

Cone 04-03 Oxidation

Kona F-4 Feldspar (Minspar 200)	17.2%
Nepheline Syenite	6.2
Ferro Frit 3124	65.8
EPK Kaolin	10.8
	100.0%
Add: Tin Oxide	4.0
Zircopax	9.0
Bentonite	2.0

This recipe is for the stiff base glaze, over which stains are applied. Add between ½ and 3+ tbsp Epsom salts to 5 gallons of glaze (flocculates the glaze for less settling and better application)

---

ate contrast. Even the math-based Della-Robbia compositions of Italy generally used blue, yellow, and green. Thinking about the color wheel and applying design concepts, I decided to go back to square one and use complimentary and analogous combinations and added black for emphasis. Gradations in wash were used for variation within this limited palette.

Always remember! If you view your efforts as an experiment and work within the context of learning, you won't set yourself up for failure. Consider a range of outcomes as successful. If you are shooting for something too specific, you probably won't get what you are looking for. The challenge of improvement will ultimately drive you to continue to make work.

Tips for designing and creating your composition:

- Start with sketches. This way, you have most of the composition worked out before you commit.
- Simplify your color palette. Too many colors can confuse the eye. Consider using one color with varying degrees of intensity along with black as a good place to start. If you are interested in becoming more elaborate with color, use a complimentary or analogous color scheme.
- Define the borders of your image area. Use a banding wheel to define the image area (figure 1). For other forms, use a light wash to define your boundaries.
- Always work light to dark. Use light washes first and create depth by gradually using more intense application of stain. Use yellow first and black last for the final emphasis of critical points in the composition. Don't forget to use the white of the glaze as your lightest value.
- Work background to foreground. Apply background colors first (figure 2). As you work with each color, move through the composition, filling in areas in the midground and foreground that have the same color (figure 3). Block out areas, leaving them white where light colored foreground imagery overlaps the background. The colored stains are like watercolors. Any marks you make continue to be visible even under layers of other colors. If you plan well, darker lines in the foreground used to develop details and that overlap lighter ones enhance the idea of perspective, as the foreground lines appear closer (figures 4 and 5).
- Work from the top of the form to the bottom. This helps to avoid smearing your previous work. If you are decorating a plate, work on the outside edges last (figure 6).

Expanding a Mid-Range Palette

by Yoko Sekino-Bové

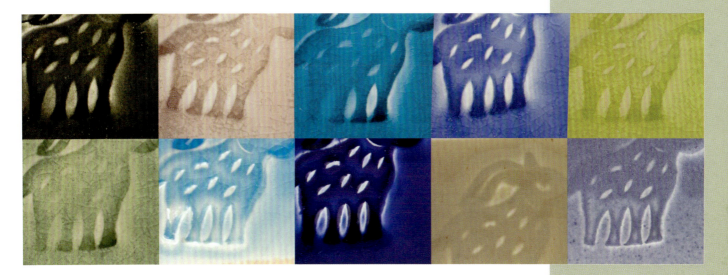

There are so many wonderful books, websites and even software that feature spectacular glaze formulas; so one may wonder why this article should be introduced to you. The focus of this research was to establish a comprehensive visual library for everyone. Rather than just providing the reader with a few promising glaze formulas, this reference is a guideline. Because it is a guide, there are some test tiles that do not provide immediate use other than the suggestion of what to avoid, or the percentages of certain chemicals that exceed the safe food-serving level, etc., but I believe that this research will be a good tool for those who wish to experiment with, and push the boundaries of, mid-range firing.

Many people may be thinking about switching their firing method from high-fire to mid-range. For instance, students who recently graduated and lost access to school gas kilns, people with a day job and those who work in their garage studios, or production potters who are concerned about fuel conservation and energy savings. This reference is intended as a tool for those people to start glaze experimentations at mid-range that can be accomplished with minimal resources.

There is no guarantee that this chart will work for everyone everywhere, since the variety between the different resources overwhelmingly affects the results, but by examining a few glazes in this chart you can speculate and make informed adjustments with your materials. This is why all the base glazes for this research use only simple materials that are widely available in the US.

Five years ago, when I was forced to switch to mid-range oxidation firing with an electric kiln, from gas-fueled reduction firing at high temperatures, most of my hard-earned knowledge in high-fire glazes had to be re-examined. Much to my frustration, many earth metal colorants exhibited completely different behaviors in oxidation firing. Also, problems in adhesion were prominent compared to high-fire glazes.

The role of oxides and carbonates used for texturing and opacifying were different as well. But compiling the available glazes and analyzing them were not enough. I felt there should be a simple chart with visual results that explained how the oxides and carbonates behave within this firing range. This motivated me to write a proposal for glaze mid-range research to the McKnight Foundation, which generously sponsors a three-month artist-in-residence program at the Northern Clay Center in Minneapolis, Minnesota.

Most of the tests presented in these experiments were executed at the Northern Clay Center from October to December in 2009 using clay and dry materials available at Continental Clay Co. The rest of the tests were completed after my residency at my home studio in Washington, Pennsylvania. For those tests, I used dry materials available from Standard Ceramics Supply Co.

Test Conditions

Clay body: Super White (cone 5–9) a white stoneware body for mid-range, commercially available from Continental Clay Co.

Bisque firing temperatures: Cone 05 (1910°F, 1043°C), fired in a manual electric kiln for approximately 10 hours.

Glaze firing temperatures: The coloring metals increment tests (page 50) were fired to cone 5 (2210°F, 1210°C) in a manual electric kiln for approximately 8 hours. The opacifier/texture metals increment tests were fired to cone 5 in an automatic electric kiln for 8 hours.

Glaze batch: Each test was 300g, with a tablespoon of epsom salts added as a flocculant.

Glazing method: Hand dipping. First dip (bottom half): 3 seconds. Second dip (top half) additional 4 seconds on top of the first layer, total 7 seconds.

Coloring Metals Increment Chart

The following colorants were tested: black nickel oxide, cobalt oxide, copper carbonate, chrome oxide, iron chromate, manganese dioxide, red iron oxide, rutile, and yellow ochre. You should note that tests with cobalt oxide and chrome oxide in high percentages were not executed due to the color predictability. Other blank tiles on the chart are because either the predictability or the percentages of oxides are too insignificant to affect the base glazes.

Depending on firing atmospheres, manganese dioxide exhibits a wide variety of colors. When fired in a tightly sealed electric kiln with small peepholes, the glaze color tends toward brown, compared to purple when fired in a kiln with

Surface Glaze & Form

Glaze base N502 with coloring oxides and carbonates

	0.1%	0.5%	1.0%	5.0%	10.0%
Copper Carbonate		N502CC05	N502CC10	N502CC50	N502CC100
Red Iron Oxide (regular)		N502ROI05	N502ROI10	N502ROI50	N502ROI100
Cobalt Oxide	N502COX0	N502COX05	N502COX10		
Chrome Oxide	N502CH01	N502CH05	N502CH10		
Manganese Dioxide		N502MD05	N502MD10	N502MD50	N502MD100
Black Nickel Oxide		N502BN05	N502BN10	N502BN50	
Iron Chromate		N502IC05	N502IC10	N502IC50	N502IC100
Rutile (powder)		N502R05	N502R10	N502R5	N502R100
Yellow Ochre		N502Y05	N502Y10	N502Y50	N502Y100

Glaze base N504 with coloring oxides and carbonates

	0.1%	0.5%	1.0%	5.0%	10.0%
Copper Carbonate		N504CC05	N504CC10	N504CC50	N504CC100
Red Iron Oxide (regular)		N504ROI05	N504ROI10	N504ROI50	N504ROI100
Cobalt Oxide	N504COX01	N504COX05	N504COX10		
Chrome Oxide	N504CH01	N504CH05	N504CH10		
Manganese Dioxide		N504MD05	N504MD10	N504MD50	N504MD100
Black Nickel Oxide		N504BN05	N504BN10	N504BN50	
Iron Chromate		N504IC05	N504IC10	N504IC50	N504IC100
Rutile (powder)		N504R05	N504R10	N504R50	N504R100
Yellow Ochre		N504Y05	N504Y10	N504Y50	N504Y100

many and/or large peepholes.

Please note that some of the oxides and carbonates in this test exceed the safety standard for use as tableware that comes in contact with food. Check safety standards before applying a glaze with a high percentage of metal oxides to food ware and test the finished ware for leaching.

Test tile numbering system: The glaze name is the first part of the identification number, followed by an abbreviation or code that stands for the colorant name. The last part is a two or three digit number referring to the percentage of colorant added.

So, for example if a test was mixed with glaze base N501, to which 1 percent cobalt oxide was added, the test tile marking would be: N501COX10.

Conclusion

This group of tests has been a great opportunity for me to study the characteristics of oxides and carbonates and how they behave at mid-range temperatures. There are scientific methods for calculating glazes and proven theories, but there are many small pieces of information that can only be picked up when you actually go through the physical experiments. It is important for us to become familiar with a glaze's behavior so that we can better utilize it. Key to that is learning both the theory and application. It is my hope that these tests will benefit many potters by helping them to expand their palette and inspire them to test the possibilities.

Glaze Base N502 with Opacifiers

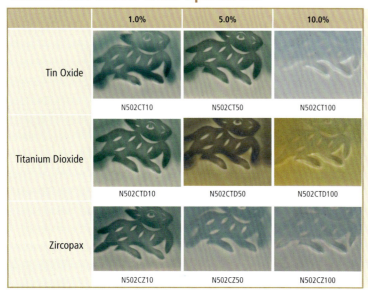

Opacifiers were added to glaze base N502 in increments. The chart at left shows which materials were added for this purpose, and the percentages tested. All glazes in this test batch also had 1% copper carbonate added to increase the visual effect of the chemicals on the glaze.

Note: Some of the oxides and carbonates did not exhibit a significant visual effect by themselves. However, sometimes a combination of more than one chemical can change the glaze characteristics and create spectacular visual effects.

Cone Six Celadons

by John Britt

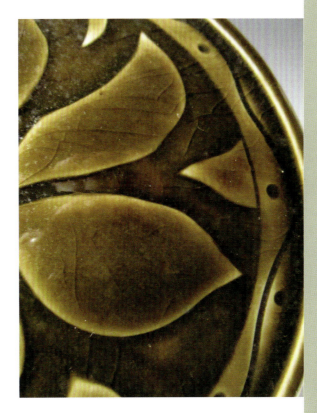

Celadon glazes are some of the most popular glazes in ceramics. In particular, transparent blue celadons have a very delicate, beautiful color that shows carving very nicely. But celadons can range from blue to blue-green to gray-blue to gray-green to green to amber, and even to white. They often have distinctive crackle patterns that are sought after but can also be craze-free.

Celadons originated in China thousands of years ago and were meant to mimic jade. The Lungchuan (Longquan) satin green celadons were important Chinese exports for over 500 years. The term "celadon" is a French word thought to have derived from a character in a French play who wore gray-green ribbons over his cloak. However, there are several competing theories of its origin.

Technically, celadons are feldspathic transparent high-fire glazes that are colored with iron and fired in reduction. This differentiates them from transparent copper greens known as Oribe, but both glaze names denote a type of ware as well as a color of glaze. Celadons were thought to have been made from the local clay body and ash, but as the glaze traveled to Korea and Japan, potters began using porcelain stone (a naturally occurring decomposed feldspathic rock).

Purists would say that a cone 6 celadon is impossible, since, by definition, it is high fired, but if we take a more practical approach and widen our definition of celadon to a transparent blue-green glaze colored with iron or other oxides, then we can include cone 6 celadons in reduction or oxidation.

Since I have worked extensively with cone 10 blue celadons, and

Recipes

Pinnell Celadon
Cone 10 reduction

Whiting	20.0%
Custer Feldspar	25.0
Grolleg Kaolin	20.0
Silica	35.0
	100.0%

Add: Tin Oxide	1.0%
Synthetic Red Iron Oxide	0.5%
Barium Carbonate*(optional)	2.0%

Pinnell Celadon Revised
Cone 6 reduction

Gerstley Borate (or substitute)	9.1%
Whiting	18.2
Nepheline Syenite	22.7
Grolleg Kaolin	18.2
Silica	31.8
	100.0%

Add: Tin Oxide	1.0%
Synthetic Red Iron Oxide	0.5%
Barium Carbonate*(optional)	0 %

Use the same firing cycle as for cone 10 gas reduction, but simply stop it at cone 6/7.

* You can substitute 1.5% strontium carbonate for the barium carbonate if you prefer.

Pinnell Celadon Revised with 0.5% synthetic red iron oxide on Grolleg porcelain.

know the principles necessary to produce that glaze, I assumed that those same principles could be used to make a cone 6 celadon. The idea is to select a glaze with high potassium (better chances for blue), high silica, small amounts of iron, and low titanium (to prevent opacifying the glaze and to prevent the iron from going green to brown). Also, a small amount of tin oxide and barium carbonate improve the blue color. Apply it thickly (two to three coats; ⅛–³⁄₁₆ inches or 3–5mm) on a clay body also low in titanium. This means that you should use Grolleg kaolin in both the clay body and the glaze recipe. Fire in an early reduction cycle, using heavy reduction (0.75–0.80 oxygen probe reading) beginning at cone 012–010 (1582–1657°F), then hold moderate reduction (0.70–0.75 oxygen probe reading) to the end of the firing. Theoretically, this should be simple, but in order to melt a glaze at cone 6 (2232°F), you need to add different fluxes, all of which have different color responses. Boron oxide is an active flux at cone 6, as are sodium, lithium, and zinc oxide, but each have their own characteristics that have to be taken to consideration. For example, zinc oxide is an excellent flux in oxidation, but if fired in reduction it volatilizes, leaving the glaze unmelted. Boron is an excellent flux in oxidation and reduction but can make the glaze cloudy. Because you have to add so much flux, sometimes up to 30% frit or Gerstley

The change from green or blue toward brown or black can happen with a very small change in the amount of iron.

borate, it is sometimes necessary to start reduction a bit earlier when firing to cone 6 or the glaze might seal over and the atmosphere will not be able to act on the iron.

So, with these considerations in mind, there are several ways to make a cone 6 blue/green celadon: move a cone 10 reduction celadon down to cone 6 reduction; test existing cone 6 bases with varying amounts of iron; or use stains to make blue/green celadons in an electric oxidation firing.

Adjusting a Cone 10 Celadon to Cone 6

Blue celadon is the most difficult color to obtain with iron, so if we start with one of those recipes, then getting a green celadon should be easy. Taking Pinnell Celadon, which is a cone 10 glaze, and substituting Nepheline Syenite for the Custer feldspar should help bring the melting temperature closer to cone 6. (Nepheline Syenite is a feldspathoid that melts at cone 6, while most

NOTE

Synthetic red iron oxide is 96–99% pure red iron, made by calcining black iron oxide in oxidation. It is then milled to 325 mesh, which makes it ideal for celadons, because it will enter the melt more quickly and thoroughly. For more, see "All About Iron," page 14, March 2011 CM.

Recipes

JOHN'S SATIN BLUE CELADON
Cone 6 reduction

Whiting	20.7%
Ferro Frit 3195	17.2
Nepheline Syenite	6.9
Grolleg Kaolin	25.9
Silica	29.3
	100.0%
Add: Tin Oxide	1.0%
Synthetic Red Iron Oxide	0.5%
For Lung Chuan (on white stoneware):	
Synthetic Red Iron Oxide	3.0%

John's Satin Blue Celadon with 0.5% synthetic red iron oxide.

John's Satin Blue Celadon with 3% synthetic red iron oxide.

Recipes

TONY HANSEN 20 x 5

Cone 6 reduction

Whiting	20.0%
Ferro Frit 3134	20.0
Custer Feldspar	20.0
Grolleg Kaolin	20.0
Silica	20.0
	100.0%
Add: Tin Oxide	1.0%
Synthetic Red Iron Oxide	0.8%
Barium Carbonate (optional)	0.8%

Tony Hansen 20x5 with 0.75% synthetic red iron oxide.

Recipes

V. C. 71

Cone 6/7 reduction

Talc	9.0
Whiting	16.0
Ferro Frit 3124	9.0
Custer Feldspar	40.0
Grolleg Kaolin	10.0
Silica	16.0
	100.0%
Add: Red Iron Oxide	0.5%

V. C. 71 with 0.5% synthetic red iron oxide

feldspar starts melting at about cone 9.) If a straight substitution doesn't cause the glaze to sufficiently melt at cone 6, which it does not in this case, start adding additional cone 6 fluxes, like frits, Gerstley borate, lithium carbonate, or zinc oxide (for oxidation only, which we'll cover later), running progressions from 1–10%. In this case, 10% Gerstley borate worked well. Alternatively, finding the proper glaze melt can be aided by glaze software, in which you get the unity molecular formula of the glaze into acceptable limits for cone 6. You will need to retotal the recipe to 100 if you add additional fluxes. After you find the surface you like, run iron progressions from 1–6% to get a celadon color you like (see tiles below).

Use an Existing Cone 6 Recipe as a Celadon Base

Since you have to do a lot of experimenting and testing to move a cone 10 glaze down to cone 6, I find that you can make an iron celadon pretty easily by just taking one of the hundreds of workable cone 6 glazes already in use with a surface you like and then, after taking out the colorants and opacifiers, running an iron progression. This will take you through a range of iron colors from blue to blue green to green to amber to tenmoku to iron saturate. Remember, always use Grolleg kaolin as the clay to keep the titanium as low as possible. The tone of the colors is dictated by the oxides that predominate in the base and the amount of iron. So a high calcium base will give different colors than a

Recipes

CHUN CLEAR
Cone 6 oxidation

Whiting	14.0%
Zinc Oxide	12.0
F-4 Feldspar (sub Minspar 200)	38.0
Kentucky Ball Clay	6.0
Silica	30.0
	100.0%
Add: Barium Carbonate (optional)	0.8%
Stains	2–3.0%
Or: Cobalt Carbonate	0.1%

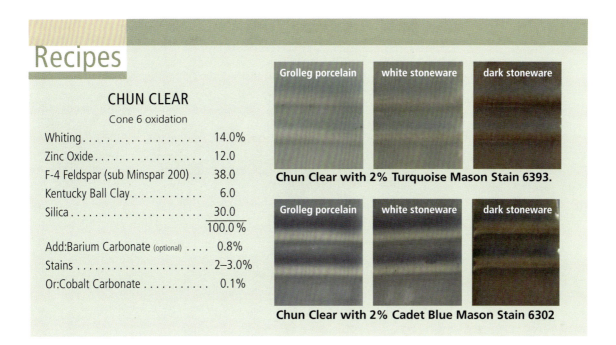

Chun Clear with 2% Turquoise Mason Stain 6393.

Chun Clear with 2% Cadet Blue Mason Stain 6302

high sodium base, regardless of firing temperature.

Use Stains to Imitate a Celadon

Using stains in a cone 6 base allows you to fire in oxidation (particularly useful for all of the folks out there firing electric kilns) even though some stains work in reduction as well. As I said earlier, zinc oxide in oxidation makes a wonderful cone 6 flux and can produce some nice colors with both oxides and stains. Many stain manufacturers recommend using 8% stain, but that makes the glaze flat and uninteresting to me, so I use very small amounts (1–3%) to keep the color delicate and transparent.

Clay Body Considerations

Finally, clay body must be considered when making cone 6 celadons. To get delicate iron blue celadons you will need to use a Grolleg clay body. Some suppliers only produce cone 10 Grolleg clay bodies, which only start to mature (less than 1% absorption) at cone 7, so you may need to fire them to cone 7. If you want a blue/green celadon, there are many cone 6 domestic porcelains that will work, as well as light and dark stonewares. It is important to mention that different clay bodies have different CTE (coefficients of thermal expansion) and that will affect the crazing or the crackle pattern. Also, expansion and contraction is affected by firing temperature, and mid-range firing (cone 5–7) spans a large temperature range (2167– 2262°F; 1186–1239°C) so maintaining consistent firings is essential.

Firing at cone 6 is a great way to both save energy and still get outstanding celadons. You can knock about three hours off of a typical cone 10 firing time, and save about a third of the fuel by firing celadons to cone 6. No one will know unless you tell them!

Bristol Glazes

by Cheryl Pannabecker

Bristol glazes were developed when the 19th century British ceramics industry moved away from using lead as its principal fluxing agent and started using zinc oxide instead. It remained the chief flux until its role was usurped by another industry advance—fritted leads. These newer glazes were easier to apply and less temperamental than the Bristol glazes.

Although the variations in surface qualities in Bristol glazes were unsuitable for industry, in the individual potter's studio they can create beautiful effects. Glaze application, thickness and thinness, its layering, the clay body, and the forms to which the Bristol glazes are applied as well as the timing and temperature of the kiln all contribute to a variety of results, earning these zinc oxide glazes their place as a mercurial glaze set.

In his 1971 book, Glaze Projects, Richard Behrens (1896–1977) explains that Bristol glazes work well for potters because of their capacity for mottling and patterning. In more contemporary glazes, we rely on zinc oxide's characteristic microcrystalline development to produce opacity in a cone 4-6 glaze. This same quality can give Bristol glazes a patterned or mottled surface. In the cone 6 glazes, it's most noticeable when colorants have been added to the glaze. The cone 4 glaze I tested flowed quite a bit and had visible patterning and mottling.

Exploring the Base Glaze

As application was initially difficult, I substituted calcined zinc oxide, which made applying the glazes easier and more successful. Brushability was a challenge with the Bristol glaze bases. Bristol IX was the most difficult, but I found adding some laundry starch to the glaze allowed an easier application.

I tested the cone 6 glazes at both cone 6 and at cone 4 on red and white stoneware, and the cone 4 glaze was tested only at cone 4. The glazes generally worked well at both temperatures, though some pinholing and pitting occurred on tests with the red stoneware body, and Bristol IX blistered and shivered off the red stoneware.

At first, I used both fast and slow glaze firing schedules when testing the glazes at cone 6 to see how they would respond. The first was a rapid firing, with no soak at the end, and the second was a crystalline-type firing schedule with a rapid 100° drop at the end of the firing followed by a three hour soak. I also did a fast cone 4 firing with a 30 minute soak at the end. I noted no significant difference in either firing, and settled on a fast firing with a 30 minute soak for the rest of my testing. This limited the amount of pinholing on the red clay. Use a clay body free of iron oxide if pinholing and other glaze defects are a consistent problem [pinholing can also be caused by a fast bisque].

Adding Color

Next, I moved on to experiment with colorants. Behrens had a Shadow Green Glaze elsewhere in the handbook that made a lovely green and happened to be Bristol VII with 1.5% green chromium oxide added, so I started there. This addition also works well in the other glaze bases.

I experimented with iron oxide, rutile, milled ilmenite, copper carbon-

1 Red stoneware with Shadow Green Glaze under Bristol X with 3% copper carbonate, fired to cone 6.

2 Bristol Glaze VII (base glaze with no colorants) on buff clay, fired to cone 4.

3 One coat Shadow Green Glaze on buff clay fired to cone 4.

4 Left: Bristol VII over Bristol X with .5% cobalt carb. Right: Bristol IX with 1.5% chromium oxide over Bristol VII. Fired to cone 4.

Surface
Glaze&Form

ate, and cobalt carbonate. Iron oxide made a glaze that was too muddy, but I found that small amounts of rutile (3%), and copper carbonate (less than 2%) worked the best. The rutile glaze was tan with significant mottling. When more than 2% copper carbonate was used, Bristols VIII and IX turned black. Bristol X was the only glaze base that allowed a nice copper green to develop, with additions of copper carbonate up to 3%. (Bristol X is the only one of these four glazes that Behrens described as bright and clear.) The addition of ilmenite or titanium encouraged a mottled surface. Cobalt carbonate produced an even, straightforward cobalt blue color, but when layered with other glazes, the coloration became dynamic.

All of the glazes were very fluid, particularly when layered together. Keep the glaze at least a half inch from the bottom of the piece, and when in doubt, use a firing slab. Glaze effects will also depend on how tightly packed the kiln is and the general mass and thickness of the ceramic pieces.

Recipes

Bristol Glaze VII
Cone 4
Lithium Carbonate	10.0%
Whiting	4.6
Zinc Oxide	22.0
EPK Kaolin	17.7
Silica	38.3
Titanium Dioxide	7.4
	100.0%

For Shadow Green Glaze, add 1.5 % green chromium oxide.

Bristol Gaze VIII
Cone 6
Lithium Carbonate	4.5 %
Zinc Oxide	12.0
Nepheline Syenite	40.5
EPK Kaolin	7.8
Silica	35.2
	100.0 %

Bristol Glaze IX
Cone 6
Lithium Carbonate	8.7%
Zinc Oxide	9.3
Nepheline Syenite	25.9
Calcined Kaolin	9.7
EPK Kaolin	11.3
Silica	35.1
	100.0 %

Bristol Glaze X
Cone 6
Lithium Carbonate	3.2 %
Zinc Oxide	6.9
Ferro Frit 25	27.3
Calcined Kaolin	7.6
EPK Kaolin	9.3
Silica	45.7
	100.0 %

Notes: I used calcined zinc—as recommended in Glaze Projects and Ferro Frit 3269 to replace Pemco Frit 25. Glazes were tested on Standard Ceramic Clay bodies: Brooklyn Red, and Buff Clay, bisqued to cone 05.

Peach Bloom Glazes

by John Britt

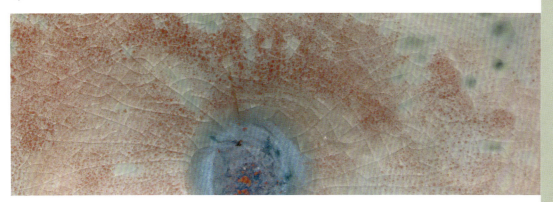

Peach Bloom glazes are some of the most delicate, beautiful, and elusive glazes known. They were used in China during the Qing dynasty (1644–1911) to decorate objects for the emperor's writing table, like water pots and ink wells, as well as decorative vases and bowls. In his definitive book Chinese Glazes, Nigel Wood lists many names for "peach bloom" glazes, like "apple red," "bean red," or "drunken beauty" for a category of glazes with various shades and a mottled surface, while "beauty's blush," "baby's face," and "peach blossom" are reserved for those with lighter tones. The number of names given to describe these glazes shows the wide variety in this magnificent glaze.

What is most intriguing is that the secrets of this glaze and firing technique have remained a mystery for centuries. At its core, peach bloom is a copper-based glaze that gives the impression of ripening fruit. So it may be a transparent green that blushes pink or a pinkish background with green or red speckling.

I have long been interested in this glaze but had never had an opportunity to pursue it fully. Then, Lindsey Elsey, a studio arts major at Appalachian State University approached me with an interest in studying copper red glazes for her senior internship. She said that, for her, copper reds were the first truly satisfying glazes she experienced in her work. She felt that, beyond their vibrant color, successful copper reds embodied the idea that if everything came together just right—the clay body, the glaze mix, application, form, firing, and cooling—then magic could happen. Although she understood that struggling with so many variables could be a frustrating process, she believed that, in the end, producing one successful pot would be worth the entire struggle.

I suggested that rather than working with the entire category of copper reds, we focus on peach blooms, which are the most difficult to achieve. Since the project seemed interesting to both of us, we agreed to work together and began by designing a testing program.

Recipes

Tom Turner Flambé 2
cone 10 reduction

Barium Carbonate	3.9%
Dolomite	5.6
Gerstley Borate	11.1
Whiting	8.3
Wood Ash (soft wood)	1.0
Zinc Oxide	1.7
Kona F-4 Feldspar	41.7
EPK Kaolin	1.7
Silica	25.0
	100.0%
Add: Tin Oxide	0.8%
Copper Carbonate	0.4%

Vase, 11 in. (28 cm) in height, wheel-thrown porcelain, with Tom Turner Flambé 2 Glaze, black copper oxide sprinkled on when wet, bisque fired to cone 06, gas oxidation fired cone 10, striking for 2 hours at 1500°F, refired in electric bisque to cone 06 along with greenware pots made of dark stoneware.

Current Literature

We found very little written on the subject of peach blooms. However, several books did have small sections: Copper Red Glazes by Robert Tichane, Stoneware Glazes by Ian Currie, Chinese Glazes by Nigel Wood and my book, The Complete Guide to High-Fire Glaze: Glazing and Firing at Cone 10. While none of these books have a definitive method, from these sources we set up a group of tests to see if we could achieve something close to ancient peach blooms.

Testing Methods

- Aging glazes to allow crystallization (Currie)
- Spraying copper/tin over a celadon glaze (Britt)
- Layering copper pigment and clear glaze (Wood)
- Sprinkling black copper oxide over glazed pots, using coarse flaked copper oxide (Tichane)
- Using Oribe glazes in oxidation firing (Britt)
- Placing pieces in saggars coated with Oribe (Britt)
- Underfiring (Britt)
- Starting reduction later, around cone 011–08 (Britt)
- Striking firing (Britt)

Due to time constraints, we knew we could not pursue all these methods, and we decided the most promising were strike firing (reduction period during the cooling) aging glazes (because I had five "old" buckets of copper reds) and sprinkling coarse copper oxide on wet glazes. While our main focus was on these avenues, we could also sample some of the other ideas without fully investigating them to see if there were some areas for future study.

We then set out to collect as many copper red recipes as we could, eventually ending up with 80 distinct recipes. As we collected recipes, we searched for as wide a variation as possible. That way, even if we did not find the perfect recipe, we would at least get something in the ball park that would hopefully lead us in the right direction.

We made 600 tiles of Helios, a Grolleg porcelain, and also threw several dozen test pieces that we would use after the initial test firings. We then made 300 gram batches of each test glaze, dipping five tiles in each glaze. Each of these was then fired in one of five different firing cycles.

Firing Cycles

Strike Firing 1 (S1) oxidized to cone 10 (2345°F or 1285°C) in a gas kiln, cooled to 1550° F, then restarted and put into reduction (0.80 on the oxyprobe) for two hours, then shut off. Missing the initial glaze reduction period on the way up causes the glaze to seal over and then the striking (reduction period during the cooling) causes only the glaze surface to reduce to reds or spotty reds. The results from this firing cycle were so good that we did another (S2) to see if we could duplicate it, but this time with even heavier reduction.

Strike Firing 2 (S2) was similar to S1, but with slightly heavier reduction (0.85 on the oxyprobe). Some

Recipes

Daly Red Titanium
cone 10 reduction

Bone Ash	1.0%
Talc	3.0
Whiting	15.0
Zinc Oxide	2.0
Ferro Frit 3110	17.0
Nepheline Syenite	35.0
Silica	27.0
	100.0 %
Add: Tin Oxide	1.5%
Titanium Dioxide	3.0%
Copper Carbonate	1.5%

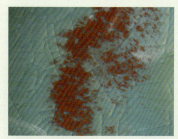

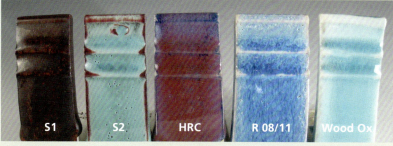

Bowl, 6 in. (15 cm) in diameter, wheel-thrown porcelain, with Daly Red Glaze (w/titanium dioxide), gas-oxidation fired cone 10, very quick cooling to 1500°F, then striking for 2 hours.

Recipes

Splotchy Lavender
cone 10 reduction

Barium Carbonate	2.0%
Lithium Carbonate	2.0
Whiting	15.0
Zinc Oxide	4.0
Hommel Frit 14	7.0
Custer Feldspar	50.0
Silica	20.0
	100.0 %
Add: Tin Oxide	1.0%
Copper Carbonate	0.6%
Bentonite	1.0%

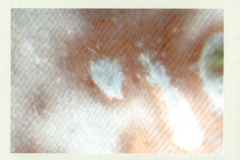

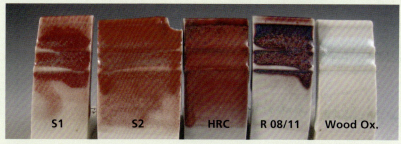

Teabowl, 5 in. (13 cm) in height, wheel-thrown porcelain, with Splotchy Lavender Glaze, black copper oxide sprinkled

Recipes

Pete's Cranberry
cone 10 reduction
Gerstley Borate	10.2%
Whiting	11.1
Custer Feldspar	73.8
Silica	4.9
	100.0%
Add: Copper Carbonate	0.4%
Tin Oxide	1.0%

Sam's Satin Celadon
cone 10 reduction
Barium Carbonate	4.0%
Dolomite	6.0
Whiting	15.5
Custer Feldspar	40.0
Silica	34.5
	100.0%
Add: Synthetic Yellow Iron Oxide	0.5%

Teabowl, 5 in. (13 cm) in height, wheel-thrown porcelain, with Pete's Cranberry Red Glaze sandwiched between Sam's Satin Celadon Glaze, gas-oxidation fired cone 10, striking for 2 hours at 1500°F.

of the pieces in this cycle came out of the kiln too dark or a flat monochrome red. This was caused by excessive reduction and meant we needed to lighten up reduction for the next trial. But in order salvage the pieces we wanted to reintroduce the spots and blue-green color, so we put them into an electric bisque kiln firing and refired them to cone 06, this was basically an oxidation soak that re-oxidized some of the copper and caused the pieces to become more visually interesting.

We did another strike firing with a very a quick cool to 1550°F (843°C). This made no difference with our color but it did cause an interesting "earthworm" or "tear" mark effect. These appear to be cracks in the glaze or piece but, in fact, are the glaze surfaces cooling rapidly while the glaze under it is still molten, causing it to shift and tear (see ex-

Recipes

Easy Red
cone 10 reduction

Gerstley Borate	10.7%
Whiting	10.7
NC-4 Feldspar	40.3
Nepheline Syenite	14.8
Spodumene	6.7
Silica	16.8
	100.0 %
Add: Tin Oxide	1.0%
Copper Carbonate	0.3%
Red Iron Oxide	0.1%

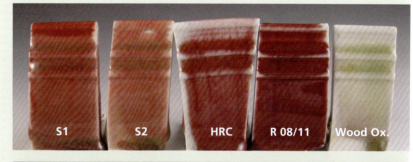

S1   S2   HRC   R 08/11   Wood Ox.

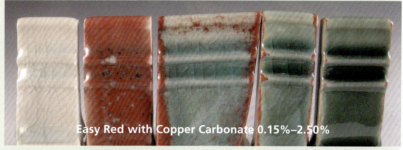

Easy Red with Copper Carbonate 0.15%–2.50%

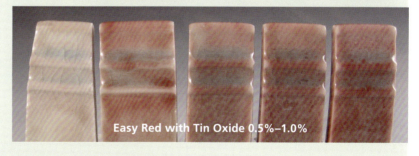

Easy Red with Tin Oxide 0.5%–1.0%

Bowl, 8 in. (20 cm) in diameter, wheel-thrown porcelain, with Easy Red Glaze, gas-oxidation fired cone 10, striking for 2 hours at 1500°F.

ample on p. 41).

Coarse copper oxide was also applied to some of the fresh raw glazed pots in these strike firings with the hope that we could better recreate the green or red spotting we saw in pictures. We made a shaker (similar to a pepper shaker) and just after we glazed our pots, but while they were still wet, sprinkled them with black copper oxide. Black copper is coarser than copper carbonate and we thought it may not completely melt, producing some green spots.

We reasoned that, since our grinding technology has greatly improved, the materials used today are much finer than those of the Qing dynasty, which may explain why you don't see much green spotting in glazes. Just as we had hypothesized, the black copper oxide produced green and black spots with green or red halos around them.

Recipes

Jeff's Red
cone 10 reduction

Barium Carbonate	4.4%
Dolomite	8.7
Whiting	8.4
Zinc Oxide	1.7
Ferro Frit 3134	8.7
Custer Feldspar	41.9
Silica	26.2
	100.0%
Add: Tin Oxide	2.6%
Copper Carbonate	0.5%
Bentonite	1.0%

Jeff's Red New Mix — S1, S2, HRC, R 08/11, Wood Ox.

Jeff's Red Aged Mix — S1, S2, HRC, R 08/11, Wood Ox.

Heavy reduction cycle (HRC) was fired to cone 022 (1100°F or 593°C), which is the beginning of dull red heat, and then put into heavy reduction (>0.80 on our oxyprobe). This was continued until cone 10 was bent to the 3 o'clock position and then the kiln was closed up and allowed to naturally cool. The results were nothing in the peach bloom range but rather the standard copper reds with very dark red to black to purple with some mottled surfaces.

R 08/11 Reduction Cycle started reduction at cone 08 and held to cone 11 (0.72 on the oxyprobe). This is a little later than the standard reduction cycle, where you start reducing copper reds at cone 010 and we also went a little hotter, to cone 11.

Wood Oxidation Firing was attempted because we had the offer of space in a firing and we thought we might learn something since the Chinese potters of the Qing dynasty fired with wood. Unfortunately, the firing was mainly oxidizing and so there were no peach blooms acquired in this firing.

Results
- The crystallization of the aged glazes showed a great difference in the outcome of the tiles. See Jeff's Red and Pete's Cranberry. The aged Splotchy Lavender also produced some very interesting mottled results.

Recipes

Norton Red
cone 10 reduction

Whiting	14.1%
Nepheline Syenite	44.4
Ferro Frit 3134	13.1
Kaolin	3.0
Silica	25.3
	100.0%
Add: Copper Carbonate	0.2%
Tin Oxide	1.0%

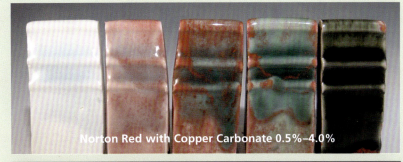

Norton Red with Copper Carbonate 0.5%–4.0%

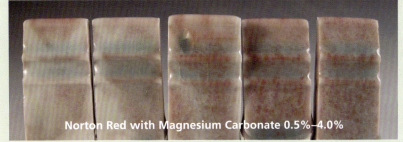

Norton Red with Magnesium Carbonate 0.5%–4.0%

- Layering a blue celadon glaze with a copper red over it, as well as sandwiching the red in between two blue celadon coats, gave some wonderful mottled blue reds (Pete's Cranberry).
- Higher amounts of tin oxide in the glaze (0.15%–2.5%) did make the glaze more milky and mottled (Easy Red).
- Higher amounts of magnesium carbonate appeared to produce more pinks (Norton Red).
- Using black copper oxide as the source of copper and/or sprinkling it on while glazing produced green and red patches (Tom Turner Flambe 2 and Splotchy Lavender).
- Additions of copper carbonate (1%–3%) in the base recipe pushed it toward green and yet still retained some red highlights (Easy Red and Norton Red).
- Refiring the over-reduced peach blooms (S2) in electric bisque with other greenware pieces of dark stoneware or earthenware gave the glazes a wonderful satin surface while re-oxidizing the red to blue with spots. This satin surface was caused by the gases (sulfur) being released from the earthenware clay. This will often happen if you mix dark greenware pieces in a majolica glaze firing (Tom Turner Flambe 2 and Splotchy Lavender).

Recipes

John's Red
cone 10 reduction

Talc	3.6 %
Whiting	13.6
Zinc Oxide	4.6
Ferro Frit 3134	9.1
Custer Feldspar	48.2
EPK Kaolin	5.5
Silica	15.5
	100.0 %
Add: Copper Carbonate	0.8 %
Tin Oxide	1.2 %

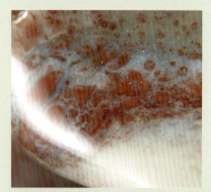

Cup, 5 in. (13 cm) in height, wheel-thrown porcelain, with John's Red Glaze outside, Pinnell Celadon inside, gas-oxidation fired cone 10, striking for 2 hours at 1500°F.

For Further Testing

Although we did achieve our goal of reproducing some beautiful peach bloom glazes, there is still a lot more to be learned about this elusive and beautiful glaze. Our testing led us to new and unusual methods of glazing and firing and opened many new roads for further testing. Layering two different copper reds and strike firing gave some more varied surfaces. Lower flux amounts made flat pink, as did under firing copper reds to cone 9 rather than cone 10. We did not get definitive results from saggar firing with Oribe or copper wash on the inside of the saggar. We also got no definitive results from spraying tin and copper over a celadon or underfiring celadons, but that's not to say we've eliminated them from testing. Through it all, it turns out that Lindsey was right: Occasionally, if everything comes together just right, magic can happen!

Steven Young Lee
West to East and Back Again

by Casey Ruble

Blue and White Jar, 23 in. (58 cm) in height, porcelain with inlaid cobalt pigments.

Trade of goods between the East and the West dates back to the early days of the Silk Routes, but it wasn't until the period of early modern colonization that Eastern motifs, styles, and subject matter became vogue in the art of the West. At the same time, Europeanizing trends appeared in the art of the East: a cross-cultural hybridization had begun.

In today's fast-paced times—when it takes less than a day to travel halfway around the world, when we can communicate with anyone, anywhere, with just the click of a mouse—such hybridization has become commonplace. Identities such as "Eastern" and "Western" are now even more fluid and complex, to the point that, say, a ceramic artist of Korean descent can be raised speaking English in Chicago, pick up Chinese during a year-long stay in China, and ultimately end up directing a residency program that draws people from across the globe to a small, mostly white town nestled in the mountains of Montana.

Such is the story of Steven Young Lee, who, after finishing his MFA at the New York College of Ceramics at Alfred University in Alfred, New York, has had varied experiences in far-flung locales—particularly in China and Korea—which have influenced his aesthetic sensibility and technical approach. "My work examines how realities are created based on experience and environment," the artist explains. "I like to question and challenge preconceptions of identity and culture."

Take, for example, Lee's Blue and White Jar—perhaps better titled Dreamy Smurf Goes to China—one of a series of pieces inspired by storage vessels from the Korean Joseon Dynasty and by the neo-Confucianist tenet to "let things be what they are." Like the other jars in this series, Blue and White Jar was created by joining two thrown parts, but without trying to create a perfectly symmetrical form. The result is an object solid yet eccentric in character, with the top half intact but the

Birds of North America, 18 in. (46 cm) in height, porcelain with inlaid cobalt and decals.

Gilded Pasture, 29 in. (74 cm) in height, porcelain with celadon glaze, mortar, and gold leaf.

bottom subtly buckled due to the weight it's been asked to support. On the surface of the jar are vignettes featuring cartoonish versions of traditional Chinese landscapes. Reclining atop one vignette's frame is the Dreamy Smurf character; another Smurf, holding a bouquet, is centered in a vignette on the back. Other jars are similarly playful, where advertising mascots for popular cereals—such as Tony the Tiger and the Trix rabbit—frolic among Asian–looking pine trees. Lee created the decoration on these jars by using an inlay technique common to traditional Korean ceramic production and fired the pieces with a clear glaze that runs slightly, pulling the inlaid cobalt pigment downward to create a greater sense of depth.

Other jars in this series are void of pop-culture surface decoration, but what they lack in humor they well make up for in seductiveness. Each is coated in layers of high-end automotive paint—Corvette "candi" red, Mercedes royal blue, Lexus pearl white—yielding an almost atmospheric visual depth due to microscopic metallic flakes suspended in the paint. Executed by professional auto body painters, the paint jobs are immaculate—a marked contrast to the intentional irregularities in the jar forms. This combination also produces an evocative dissonance between age-old techniques and technologically advanced ones, as well as between the unique original and standardized production.

References to mass production crop up in Lee's other works as well—most notably in sculptures involving multiple bunny rabbits of the sort one might find in the children's aisle of a dollar store. Lee used a press mold to produce close to a hundred of these porcelain bunny forms, which are solid in color and have bulbous bodies and blank ovals for eyes. In some pieces, groups of bunnies are placed on large circular or rectangular tiers, recalling store-window displays. Other pieces consist of a single rabbit head, with various surface treatments such as a celadon glaze with hand-carved flower motif. One can't help but compare these works to Jeff Koons' stainless steel Rabbit (1986), but Lee's pieces have an added meaning: Whereas Koons' sculpture resides firmly in the realm of American pop culture, Lee's rabbits reference not only Western Easter bunnies but also the Chinese zodiac. In fact, it was the latter reference that first compelled Lee to make the pieces. "When I first arrived in China," he says, "people kept asking me what my birth year was. I told them I was born in the year of the rabbit, and they would make assumptions about me based on that. It wasn't until much later that I realized I'd calculated my birth year incorrectly—I'd been using the Western Gregorian calendar, but according to the lunar calendar that Eastern cultures use,

***Instinct and Consequence**, 81 in. in height, porcelain, gold plating, glaze.*

I was actually born in the year of the tiger. I was fascinated by the difference between the characteristics of those two signs and how it changed people's initial perception of me."

This kind of "bilingualism" is also evident in Birds of North America (2007), another set of Joseon-dynasty-inspired jars. Here, Lee placed decals of birds native to Western countries (cardinals, blue jays) atop inlaid pine trees executed in the style of Japanese and Chinese ink painting. Like Granary Jar and Blue and White Jar, at first glance these pieces appear to be typical examples of chinoiserie; it is only on further inspection that one realizes that Lee is not merely appropriating a visual style but rather integrating various visual languages; the separate elements remain relatively autonomous but engage in communication with one another. One might draw a parallel between this and immigrants' experiences of assimilation versus integration—the former being wholesale absorption into the dominant culture; the latter, adaptation to that culture but without abandoning one's native identity.

Lee puts a personal spin on this idea in his series of pagoda-topped vessels inspired by Chinese Han dynasty spirit jars. These pieces initially seem indecipherable from their 2000-year-old predecessors, yet closer scrutiny reveals several of the pagodas bear an uncanny resemblance to the beehive brick kilns that still stand on the grounds of the Archie Bray Foundation.

Custom Colors
by Steven Young Lee

In some of my pieces, I have worked with other professional craftsmen to execute parts of the process. For instance, in the series of jars inspired by the Joseon Dynasty I outsourced the surface treatment to Travis Johnston at Economy Auto Body, a local automotive body shop in Helena, Montana, that specialize in custom paint jobs on cars and speedboats. They use a basecoat/clearcoat system allowing me to choose from a line of DuPont Chromabase pigments that can be matched to a specific make and model of car (BMW Black, Lexus Pearlescent White, etc). Mica flakes and additional clear coats were also added to increase the surface depth.

It was important to find the right people who could understand the ideas and importance of the finish. Their experience with specialty jobs helped them relate to my vision for the pieces and complete them effectively. The ability to communicate ideas became crucial to the execution of this work.

Top to bottom: Blue Jar (Mercedes Bahama Blue Pearl Metallic F2332), Candi Red Jar (Laser Red Metallic Tri Coat B9407), Pearlescent White Jar (Lexus White Pearl Metallic L9018), Yellow Jar (Chrysler Prowler Yellow B9854), Black Jar (BMW Black Sapphire Pearl Metallic M9999), each 21 in. (53 cm) in height, porcelain with automotive paint: DuPont Basecoat Pigments followed by DuPont 62-7779 clear coat with Mica Medium Coarse Flakes.

Throughout much of his work, Lee embraces the irregularities and mishaps that generally are seen as making an object worthless. The artist often intentionally cracks pieces or fires them to the point of breaking. In some cases he carves imagery on the inside of the vessel as well as the outside, letting viewers know that they are actually supposed to be able to see the interior. Other times he fills in the cracks with a textured mortar that is then covered in gold leaf. Lee thus challenges the identity of the vessel as a functional object meant to contain something. Indeed, the idea of containment—or lack thereof—is a key component in all of Lee's work. Transgressing boundaries of all types—geographic, cultural, visual, functional—Lee allows a spilling out of meanings as diverse as the experiences that inspired them.

Laying it on Thick

by Steven Young Lee

For the inlay pieces, I draw into the surface of the leather-hard clay with a set of small woodcarving knives. The timing and choice of clay is crucial to get a clean line; the porcelain provides a smooth clean surface to draw on, but if the clay is too dry the edges will tear and crumble. The drawing takes two to three days, during which time the work is kept in a plastic tent to maintain humidity and protect the drawn lines.

In the traditional Korean inlay process, the slip is added to the leather-hard piece and then scraped off when dry to reveal the inlaid colored clays. I've tried this method in the past but found that I would often lose some of the detail in my drawing. I now bisque-fire my pieces after carving, sand the edges down with sandpaper, and then fill in the carved lines with cobalt/porcelain slip. After the slip dries on the surface, I scrape off the excess with a metal rib. This slip is reconstituted and used again. The surface is wiped clean of excess slip and then glazed with a clear glaze.

Recipes

White Slip Base
(cone 9/10)

Nepheline Syenite	15 %
EPK Kaolin	15
Grolleg Kaolin	30
XX Sagger Clay	25
Silica	15
	100 %

Colors for inlay slip:
Blue: Cobalt Oxide 1–2%
Black: Cobalt Oxide 4%, Manganese Dioxide 4%, Red Iron Oxide 6%, Chrome Oxide 2%

After a piece has been carved and bisque fired, inlay slip is applied and allowed to dry before it is removed with a metal rib. This allows Lee to preserve the precision of the carving.

Your Source for Inspired Techniques

THE CERAMIC ARTS HANDBOOK SERIES

  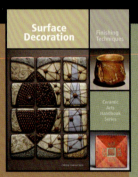 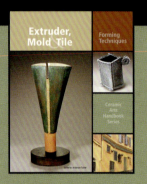
  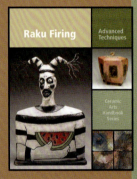 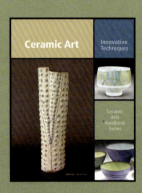
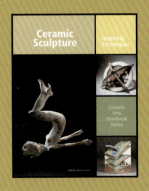  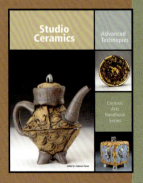 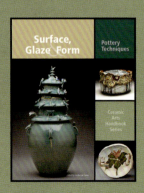

ceramicartsdaily.org/books
866-721-3322